SIMPLE AND SPEEDY
WHOLEFOOD COOKING

For the cook who wants to spend the minimum of time in
the kitchen and yet enjoy all the benefits of wholefood
cooking, here is an abundance of interesting alternatives and
advice for quick and delicious dishes.

SIMPLE AND SPEEDY WHOLEFOOD COOKING

Time-saving Recipes for All Occasions

by

JANET HUNT

Illustrated by Ivana T. Cooke

THORSONS PUBLISHERS LIMITED
Wellingborough, Northamptonshire

First published 1982
Fourth Impression 1985

British Library Cataloguing in Publication Data

Hunt, Janet. *1942-*
    Simple and speedy wholefood cookery.
    1. Cookery (Natural foods)
    I. Title
    641.5'637   TX741

    ISBN 0-7225-0752-6

Printed in Great Britain by
Richard Clay (The Chaucer Press) Ltd,
Bungay, Suffolk

CONTENTS

Wholefoods, quite simply, are foods in their natural state – nothing added, nothing taken away. In this age of mass-production foods, wholefoods are not always easy to obtain. But as nutritionists and doctors become increasingly convinced of their value in building and maintaining health, so their availability is fast improving.

Include as many natural, unadulterated foods as you can in your day to day eating pattern, and discover not just exciting new tastes and a fresh approach to mealtimes, but better health too.

1.
CRAFTINESS IN THE KITCHEN

Awareness of the importance of eating wholesome, natural foods has never been more widespread. Thanks to the media, to outspoken doctors and nutritionists, and to an education system that encourages the enquiring mind, the link between good health and good eating is now appreciated by a fast-growing number of people of varying ages, from all walks of life.

No longer is it considered cranky to care – it just makes sense – and, as the importance of wholefoods is recognized, suspicion about convenience foods is rife. The recent reliance on sachets, packets and tins is at last being seen for what it is – not just lazy and costly, but possibly dangerous too.

Far removed from their natural state, what these foods lose in the refining process is replaced by additives, preservatives, colouring and flavouring – in short, chemicals that make them quick to cook, easy to digest and about as nutritious as the packaging in which they are presented!

Why, then, doesn't everybody eat wholefoods? In these days of rush and hurry, one of the main reasons given for not switching to a healthier eating plan is quite simply lack of time, and it *can* be a very real problem. A new way of eating needs to be thought out carefully – meals must be approached in a different way so that nutrients are balanced and complete.

Ingredients must be assembled so that dishes look appetizing and taste good, especially when they are being served to a family who may be unfamiliar with wholefoods and nervous about them. It must be admitted that many wholefoods take longer to cook than their refined counterparts – at least until you learn how to cut corners in the kitchen. And *that* is what this book aims to tell you.

But first, a few words about what not to eat if you intend to switch to a healthier eating plan. Aim, if you can, to give up refined foods such as white bread and flour, white sugar, polished rice, pasta made from refined wheat – all of these lack fibre (now known to be vital to health) as well as many nutrients.

Flesh foods have no real place in a wholefood diet, most meats coming from animals reared in factory farms and treated with hormones and antibiotics, many of which may be passed on to accumulate in your body. Animal fats such as butter, cream and many cheeses have long been known to contribute to obesity, and have also been linked with heart disease. In recent years they have become even more suspect for their role in the cholesterol controversy. Although they do have a lot to offer nutritionally, their use should be kept to a minimum.

Finally, aim to restrict your use of any foods that you know to be full of chemicals. Learn to read labels. If the list of additives is long, put it back on the shelf. If it contains white sugar, white flour, etc. (and most convenience foods do!), forget it. Look carefully and you will probably find some tinned, dried or packaged foods that contain fewer additives and a little more in the way of nutrients – these are the ones to buy and keep at the back of your cupboard for those emergencies when you have to produce a meal out of thin air. Frozen foods, too, can have a part to play in a wholefood diet – but it's a small part. Base your eating on fresh and natural foods, and you can use the occasional convenience food without coming to too much harm!

These, then, are the foods on which you should stock up:

Nuts and Seeds
A high-energy food and a major source of protein in the wholefood diet. As they are so rich they can be used sparingly. Buy them in their raw state rather than fried, flavoured and devitalized, and in small amounts so that they are fresh. Try

almonds, hazels, brazils, walnuts, pine kernels; also sunflower, sesame and pumpkin seeds. Peanuts (especially high in protein) and cashews (less rich but still valuable) are not actually part of the nut family, but are usually termed as such. Chestnuts are a good source of carbohydrate.

Pulses

Not so rich in protein, but the value can be increased by combining them with other ingredients. Pulses also offer B vitamins, calcium, phosphorus, magnesium and iron. There are over twenty varieties to choose from – the most popular being soya beans, haricot beans, black-eye peas, chick peas, butter beans, whole peas, kidney beans, lima beans. Especially quick-cooking are lentils, split peas, aduki and mung beans.

Grains

Conventional diets make little use of these, and miss out on a remarkably good value-for-money food. They are simple to cook, versatile, subtly flavoured and very satisfying. The best known are wheat berry, barley, rye, oats, bulgur, buckwheat, millet, and of course, rice, many of them taking only a very short time to cook. Again look out for the unrefined version. Brown rice, for example, contains minerals and B vitamins in its outer husk – the part that is removed from white rice!

Cheese

An exceptionally high protein food which can also be high in fat – don't use too much at one time. Try all varieties, including the many now available from abroad. Strict vegetarians can obtain cheese made with vegetable rather than animal rennet, and many soft cheeses are also made without animal rennet. Processed cheeses contain more additives and water than actual cheese, so are best avoided. One time-saving tip: grate any stale hard cheese when you have a few minutes to spare and keep it in a screw-topped jar in the fridge, ready for instant use when you're cooking in a hurry.

Milk

Use in limited amounts – it's intended to be fed to growing babies who eat no other protein-rich foods, and is therefore highly concentrated. Because of this, a milk-rich diet can cause allergies and other problems for adults. Try it in other forms – yogurt is ideal in a health-building diet as it's easier to digest, low in fat. (As a change, you may like to try one of the various plant milks now available. Made from soya beans, they are surprisingly good and can be used as ordinary milk.)

Fats and Oils

Butter, though high in fat and cholesterol, is usually a fairly natural food, and can be used, but sparingly. Try to substitute a low-cholesterol polyunsaturated margarine as part of your day-to-day eating pattern though. In cooking, use vegetable oils whenever possible, the best being sunflower, safflower, sesame, corn, soy, peanut and olive.

Bread

The popularity of bread made from 100 per cent wholemeal flour is the success story of the last decade. Once only available from health food stores, it can now be bought at most bakers and supermarkets. As bread plays such an important role in most people's eating habits, it is important to use wholemeal whenever possible – it supplies nutrients and fibre, is more filling and therefore less fattening, and tastes deliciously different from the white cotton-wool variety! Do be sure you are getting real wholemeal bread, though, and not the kind of brown bread that is made with refined white flour that has been dyed.

Flour

Again, try to get used to using 100 per cent wholemeal flour, (81 per cent is a finer version and may suit you better, at least until you get used to using coarser flour in your baking and cookery). Refined white flour has little to offer in the way of nourishment and taste.

Fruit and Vegetables
You probably already eat these foods in reasonable amounts, but in a wholefood diet they feature more often and in a variety of guises. Learn to be adventurous with them, making them the centre-piece of your meal rather than an accompanying mouthful. Obviously, the fresher they are the better, so buy in small amounts and use them up quickly. Over-cooking will reduce their food value *and* taste – in fact, it's a good idea to eat them raw as often as possible. Stir-frying is a quick and easy way to cook most vegetables, so is steaming. As most of the nutrients lie just beneath the skin, buy a stiff-bristled brush and scrub them clean rather than peeling – then chop them finely, cook them quickly, and enjoy their flavour.

Eggs
These are especially quick and easy to prepare, and packed with goodness. Watch out, though, that you don't have too many as the yolks are especially rich in cholesterol. Battery eggs, produced scientifically, come from chickens fed on chemicals and sometimes synthetic dyes to make the yolks a good colour. Look out for free-range eggs, they're worth the little extra they may cost.

More Valuable Wholefoods for Your Store Cupboard

Vegetable Stock Cubes These are made up in minutes and save the day when you haven't got any fresh stock to hand.

Tahini A butter made from hulled sesame seeds and packed with protein.

Nut Butters Also protein-rich and invaluable, not just for sandwiches but as a quick way to thicken soups and flavour savoury dishes.

Miso A paste made from fermented soya beans, wholewheat or barley and sea salt.

Tamari A soy sauce that is actually a by-product of miso. It has a rich, salty taste.

Wholemeal Pasta This is now available in a variety of shapes. It is delicious, nutritious, very quick-cooking and versatile – a real 'convenience' food for wholefooders.

Raw Cane Sugar This food has some important minerals, but its use should still be kept to a minimum. Again, don't be fooled into buying white sugar that has been dyed brown. Read the pack: if it's raw, the country of origin will be stated, and probably the word 'raw' too. If there's a list of ingredients it means the sugar has been manufactured!

Blackstrap Molasses This is another important source of sweetness – a rich source of most of the B vitamins, in particular B_6, and also iron, copper, calcium and magnesium. A taste well worth acquiring.

Honey This is one of the most easily digested forms of sweetening, and its delicate flavour can make all the difference to a dish. Like all forms of sweetening it should be used sparingly.

Sea Salt Preferable to refined salt because it contains some minerals and trace elements, but don't rely too heavily on it as salt *can* become addictive. (It can also ruin the delicate taste of natural ingredients).

Tofu Is a white curd made from soya beans. Many (if not most) wholefood and health food shops now sell it, some offering a choice between a firmer and silken version. High in protein, low in saturated fats and calories, cholesterol-free and amazingly inexpensive, tofu is an excellent food. Its bland taste needs to be creatively treated to make it more interesting, but once you've got the idea you'll find its versatility makes it an ideal ingredient for both savoury and sweet dishes.

Textured Vegetable Protein (T. v. p.) One of the few 'scientific' foods that has a place in a wholefood diet. Soya meat is a nutritious, protein-rich, low-calorie food that is also inexpensive, easy to store, quick to cook. Its bland flavour can be livened up in a wide variety of ways, and also makes it very versatile.

Bean Sprouts Keep them in the fridge, not the cupboard! These are best grown at home – and they're easy to do – but nowadays they are also available in many shops. They are full of vitamins, plus protein and other nutrients, and provide an easy way to add crunch and interest to savoury dishes and salads.

Dried Fruits Use these instead of the tinned variety as they are rich in natural sugars and minerals. They are also very concentrated, so don't have too many at one time (prunes are the lowest in calories!) Try to obtain the sun-dried unadulterated variety.

Granola and Muesli The wholefooder's breakfast cereals that start any day well, these are also invaluable as quick toppings to sweet dishes and can be added to baking for new textures and tastes. They make a satisfying snack, eaten by the handful (most children prefer granola this way!)

Wheat Germ, Bran, Soya Flour and Dried Milk Powder These are the only 'additives' you should allow in your kitchen! These foods are all packed with goodness and can be added to just about anything you are preparing for an instant boost in nutritional content. All are best used fresh, so buy in small quantities and store in the cool.

So now you know what's what – what's best, what's cheapest, what's quickest to cook. Now it's time to set up your kitchen. You'll soon discover that a well organized and planned kitchen is a major key to getting more done in less time.

is a major key to getting more done in less time.

You need a good work surface, one that is at a handy height, in a convenient position, and clutter-free. You need all your ingredients to be stored somewhere accessible, preferably in see-through jars with air-tight screw-on tops. A good herb and spice rack is invaluable, (better still, a box of growing herbs on your window ledge). A well-designed vegetable rack that you keep full of basic ingredients (to be used in rotation), has pride of place in a wholefood kitchen.

The right kitchen equipment is obviously important, but don't think that the more you have, the better. In fact, it's advisable to limit your tools to the minimum – who wants to be bothered with complicated gadgets when time is limited? These are the essentials – with them you can do just about everything you'll want to do:

A selection of good quality knives, kept sharp
Heavy-based pans in a range of sizes
Chopping board
Measuring jug
Quality grater
Small grinder/liquidizer
Steamer (the best is a simple stainless steel contraption
    that fits into most sizes of saucepan)
Hand vegetable chopper
Wooden spoon
Pressure cooker – not absolutely necessary, but invaluable as a
    way to save time and fuel, especially when cooking such
    things as beans.

Once your kitchen is organized and ready for action, it's time to consider making another change – and that is a change of attitude. The way you cook (and the amount of time you spend doing it) is a direct result of how you think about food, what you consider a good and balanced meal, whether or not you are willing to adapt and compromise. If, for example, a meal to you means meat and two veg., plus a dessert, maybe with a starter, you will spend a good deal of time preparing your food – and washing up after it. If you choose, instead, to pile a lot of ingredients into one casserole, add a simple protein in the form of grated cheese or nuts, and finish with fresh fruit, your meal will be well balanced nutritionally as well as quick to cook.

Simplicity is all-important if you're trying to reduce the time you spend in the kitchen. Use fresh and tasty ingredients and there's no need to fancy them up. Instead of two vegetables with a savoury dish, have a salad (and don't just use traditional salad ingredients – it is quite likely that the vegetables you intended to cook will taste great raw!). Instead of cooking potatoes or rice separately, combine it with the main dish. Or have a slice or two of wholemeal bread as your starch.

It is well worth making a conscious effort to cook more than you need, especially of slow-cooking ingredients such as grains and beans. They will keep well in the fridge, losing only the minimum amount of their original nutritional value, and providing the makings of instant meals a day or two later. Cooked vegetables can be added to savouries or salads. The stock, of course, can be used for soup, or in a sauce. Cold fritters can be broken up and fried with cabbage and potatoes, cold pizza can be put into a lunch box, cold omelette can be chopped up and sprinkled over a salad or rice savoury. Just about anything can be thrown into the blender to make a soup or sauce. The alternatives are endless. Left-overs used to play an important role in the kitchen, but in recent (more affluent) years they have tended to become discarded. Take a fresh look at what you can do with them, and you'll understand why they held grandmother in such good stead.

Experiment, too, with all-in-one cookery. For example, the white sauce given on page 31 can be cooked by simply putting all the ingredients together in a pan and heating gently whilst whisking continually. It takes less time than the traditional way, and is considerably easier, and if the taste is slightly different (*sautéeing* the flour adds flavour), you can add seasoning or other ingredients to make up for it. Try making cakes and biscuits in the same way – everything in together.

Give a little extra thought to planning a week or two of possible menus, and you'll save even more time. Just having a rough idea of what you might serve means you can cook double quantities when necessary, can shop for the week instead of going back and forth, and can eliminate last minute panics when you're hungry and tired and fresh out of ideas! On the subject of shopping, do buy in bulk whenever possible. Many wholefood ingredients can be stored for long periods of time, providing you make sure they're fresh when you bring them home and store them well. Having them handy makes meal-preparing so much easier.

One final tip: enjoy yourself in the kitchen. Whether you love cooking but just don't have enough time to potter with the pots and pans, or hate it and just can't get out of there quickly enough, you should remember that you are doing much more than just preparing something to eat. You are doing something very positive to keep yourself and your family in tiptop health. Don't see cooking as a chore – see it as a challenge, and an enjoyable one at that. Don't worry about whether or not everything will taste as it should – if you're using wholesome ingredients it's going to taste good even if it's not what you expected. And don't be *too* concerned about details – exact measurements, a herb or seasoning, a missing ingredient. Learn to judge rather than measure, to experiment rather than follow exactly, to innovate as you go along. That's what creative cookery is all about. It's also the way to cut corners of your own. And when you've learned to do that, you can pass this book to someone else!

Note: All recipes will serve 4 people unless otherwise stated. Timing of recipes can only be very approximate since different people work at different paces – and so do ovens!

2
SOUPS ASSORTED

Supermarkets are full of soups that can be made effortlessly, in minutes. Tinned soups, packet soups, boxed soups may be convenient but are they nutritious? Hardly. Why have the artificial version when you can have the real thing for little more effort and decidedly less money?

Home-made soups are all things to all people. Thick and hearty, they are a man-sized meal in themselves. Smooth, creamy, delicately flavoured, they are a gourmet's delight. Light soups are excellent appetizers and will tempt jaded palates, finicky children, and older folk concerned about indigestion.

A few tips: The best vegetable stock is the water in which vegetables have been cooked – it's packed with minerals! – but if you have none handy, use vegetable stock cubes instead. When using flour, both 81 per cent and 100 per cent wholemeal are fine. The results will vary in taste and texture slightly, so try them, then use which you and your family prefer. The smaller you cut your vegetables, the quicker your soup will cook – they can even be grated and then cooked in minutes. Most of the recipes given here can be served after a short cooking time, in which case the ingredients will be crisp and crunchy, or cooked longer for a mushy consistency; for a smooth soup *purée* put the vegetables in a blender or press them through a sieve. And don't forget this is an ideal way to give left-overs a new lease of life!

Garnishes to add texture, flavour, goodness: grated cheese or cream cheese balls; a spoonful or two of cream, soured cream, yogurt or tahini; any dried or fresh chopped herbs; thin slices of raw leeks, tomatoes, mushrooms, tiny florets of raw cauliflower; a few cooked peas or beans; orange and lemon slices or peel; *croûtons* made by shallow-frying cubes of wholemeal bread; mashed potato to thicken the soup; a pinch of paprika, chilli powder, nutmeg or curry powder; lightly roasted almond or peanut flakes; fried *Shredded Wheat* or *All Bran*; chopped hard-boiled egg.

AFRICAN BEAN SOUP
Time: 15 minutes

12 oz (350g) cooked kidney beans
2 large tomatoes
1 large onion
1 green pepper
⅓ pint (200ml) coconut milk (made with 2 oz (50g)
   desiccated coconut or 2 oz (50g) creamed coconut)
1 teaspoonful curry powder
Sea salt to taste

1. Prepare the coconut milk either by pouring boiling water over the desiccated coconut and leaving for 15 minutes before draining or by dissolving the creamed coconut in the boiling water.

2. Slice the vegetables.

3. Combine the drained beans, vegetables, coconut milk, curry powder and salt.

4. Bring to the boil then simmer for approximately 10 minutes, or until the soup thickens. Add more water if necessary.

MILLET SOUP
Time: 30 minutes

2 medium onions
2 medium carrots
About ¼ medium white cabbage
4 oz (100g) millet
1 tablespoonful vegetable oil
2 pints (1 litre) water
Seasoning and herbs to taste

1. Remove skin from the onions and peel the carrots; chop all vegetables finely.

2. *Sauté* briefly in the hot oil; add the millet and cook gently for 5 more minutes.

3. Add the water, seasoning and herbs, and bring to the boil; cover the pan and simmer until all ingredients are cooked (approximately 20 minutes).

POTATO AND CELERY SOUP
Time: 20 minutes

2 heads celery
6 medium potatoes
1 oz (25 g) polyunsaturated margarine
1½ pints (¾ litre) water
Seasoning to taste

1. Chop the celery into tiny pieces and *sauté* in the melted margarine.

2. Peel and chop or grate the potatoes, then add to the celery with the water.

3. Bring to the boil, then simmer until vegetables are cooked; add seasoning.

4. Serve hot with a sprinkling of parsley or paprika for colour, or cold with a little yogurt.

MINESTRONE
Time: 40 minutes

1 tin haricot beans
2 tablespoonsful olive oil
1½ pints (¾ litre) water or vegetable stock
About 1 lb (450g) mixed vegetables (a traditional
    combination is onion, carrots, leeks, turnips, celery,
    peas)
2 oz (50g) wholemeal macaroni
1 garlic clove
Seasoning to taste
Grated Parmesan cheese

1. Clean all the vegetables and chop into small pieces (except the peas).

2. Heat the oil and *sauté* the vegetables with the crushed garlic for 10 minutes.

3. Add the water, peas, drained beans, macaroni and seasoning. Bring to the boil, cover and simmer for 20 minutes.

4. Serve with the grated cheese.

TOMATO SOUP WITH RICE
Time: 35 minutes

1 lb (450g) fresh tomatoes
1 large onion
2 sticks celery
1 oz (25g) polyunsaturated margarine
4 oz (50g) cooked brown rice
1½ pints (¾ litre) vegetable stock
Seasoning and herbs to taste

1. Skin and chop the tomatoes and onion; cut the celery into pieces.

2. *Sauté* the vegetables in the melted margarine for a few minutes.

3. Pour in the stock, add the seasoning and herbs and bring to the boil.

4. Cover the pan and simmer the vegetables for about 20 minutes.

5. Optional – for a smooth soup, sieve or liquidize the vegetables, then return to the saucepan.

6. Add the rice and cook gently for 5 minutes to heat through.

Variation: Use any left-over grains in this soup – millet, buckwheat, wholewheat berries are all delicious.

CASHEW AND CARROT SOUP

Time: 25 minutes

2 oz (50g) cashew pieces
1 small onion
8 oz (225g) carrots
2 oz (50g) wholemeal flour
2 pints (1 litre) vegetable stock
2 oz (50g) skimmed milk powder
1 oz (25g) polyunsaturated margarine
Seasoning to taste
Single cream – optional

1. Use a grinder to powder the cashew pieces.

2. Melt the margarine and *sauté* the chopped onion and carrot in it for a few minutes.

3. Add the flour and cashew powder to the vegetables and cook gently for a few minutes until lightly browned.

4. Mix the milk powder into the vegetable stock, season, then pour into the pan with the other ingredients.

5. Bring to the boil then simmer for 15 minutes. If using cream, spoon some into each bowl and pour soup over it.

WATERCRESS SOUP
Time: 10 minutes

2 bunches watercress
1 large onion
2 oz (50g) mushrooms
1 tablespoonful vegetable oil
1½ pints (¾ litre) water
2-3 teaspoonsful yeast extract

1. Fry the sliced onion gently in the hot oil for a few minutes.

2. Add the washed, dried and roughly chopped watercress and water and bring to the boil.

3. Dissolve the extract in the boiling water, then lower the heat; add the thinly sliced mushrooms, and simmer for about 5 minutes.

SPINACH EGG SOUP WITH BEAN SPROUTS
Time: 10 minutes

8 oz (225g) young spinach
2 eggs
2 pints (1 litre) vegetable stock
½ teaspoonful cornflour
Soy sauce
4 tablespoonsful fresh bean sprouts

1. Heat the stock to boiling point; beat the eggs with the cornflour.

2. Slowly pour the eggs through a sieve into the boiling stock; lower the heat and simmer for 1 or 2 minutes.

3. Add the washed, shredded spinach and bean sprouts and cook for just 1 or 2 minutes more.

4. Serve at once with a little soy sauce added.

CREAMY LENTIL SOUP

Time: 20 minutes

8 oz (225g) small red lentils
2 pints (1 litre) water
1 tablespoonful tarragon
Seasoning to taste
2 oz (50g) cream cheese

1. Wash the lentils, then add to the water with the tarragon and bring to the boil.

2. Simmer covered for 10 to 15 minutes until cooked.

3. Remove from the heat, season to taste, and stir in the cheese until completely dissolved.

Variation: A creamy soup can also be obtained by replacing the cream cheese with single cream, yogurt, soured cream or buttermilk.

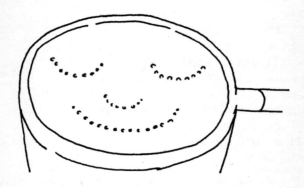

MISO SOUP
Time: 25 minutes

1 large onion
2 large carrots
¼ medium cabbage or 8 small brussels sprouts
4 oz (100g) tofu, cubed
2 pints (1 litre) water
1 tablespoonful miso
Seasoning to taste

1. In the hot oil, carefully *sauté* the peeled, chopped vegetables and the cubed tofu until the tofu is lightly browned.

2. Add the water and simmer for about 15 minutes.

3. Pour a little of the water into a small bowl and dilute the miso. Return to the saucepan and cook for 5 more minutes on a low heat. Taste and season if necessary.

AVOCADO SOUP
Time: 5 minutes

2 large ripe avocados
2 pints (1 litre) skimmed milk
2 oz (50g) polyunsaturated margarine
Seasoning to taste
Pinch of paprika

1. Mash the avocados.

2. Combine all the ingredients in a saucepan and heat gently without boiling. At the same time, beat the soup until light and frothy in texture.

3. Serve at once, topped with a little paprika.

SESAME CABBAGE SOUP
Time: 20 minutes

1 medium cabbage
1 large onion
2 oz (50g) polyunsaturated margarine
2 pints (1 litre) water
2 tablespoonsful oatmeal
2 tablespoonsful tahini (sesame paste)
Seasoning to taste
Parsley

1. Chop the onion and shred the cabbage finely; *sauté* them together in the melted margarine, taking care that they do not brown.

2. Add the boiling water and gradually stir in the oatmeal.

3. Simmer until the cabbage is cooked.

4. Remove from the heat; season, add sesame paste and combine well. Check that the paste has dissolved completely.

5. Serve topped with parsley.

Variation: A more traditional soup can be made by replacing the sesame paste with soured cream, single cream or yogurt.

Cold Soups for Hot Days

YOGURT AND CUCUMBER SOUP
Time: 10 minutes

1 large cucumber
2 small cartons plain yogurt
1 tablespoonful chopped fresh dill
⅓ pint (200 ml) milk
Seasoning to taste
Pinch of paprika

1. Wash and dry the cucumber, then finely grate it. Sprinkle with salt and set it aside for a short time, then rinse.

2. Combine the cucumber with the yogurt, herbs and seasoning and enough milk to make the soup a smooth consistency.

3. Serve chilled, topped with wafer-thin slices of cucumber and a light sprinkling of paprika.

GAZPACHO (in blender)

Time: 10 minutes

1 lb (450g) fresh tomatoes
1 medium cucumber
1 small green pepper
2 or 3 spring onions or 1 small onion
1 garlic clove
A little vegetable oil
Lemon juice
Seasoning to taste

1. Peel and chop the tomatoes, cucumber, pepper and onions into small pieces.

2. Put into a blender with the crushed clove of garlic and oil and combine well.

3. Adjust the consistency of the soup by adding a little water, if necessary. Season, and squeeze in some lemon juice.

4. Serve chilled with some diced cucumber on top.

SWEET CORN CHOWDER
Time: 15 minutes

1 medium onion
1 oz (25 g) polyunsaturated margarine
1 oz (25 g) wholemeal flour
1 pint (½ litre) milk
½ pint (¼ litre) vegetable stock
1 tin creamed sweet corn
Lemon juice
Seasoning to taste
1 small green pepper

1. Melt the margarine and lightly fry the sliced onion without burning.

2. Add the flour and cook briefly.

3. Stir in the milk and stock and bring to the boil. Add the sweet corn and cream sauce. Simmer for 10 minutes.

4. Season, squeeze in a little lemon juice and chill thoroughly.

5. Serve with some finely chopped green pepper.

3.
TOPPING SAUCES –
SAUCY TOPPINGS

In a conventional cookery book sauces rarely receive the attention they deserve. They are thought of as a 'little extra' that maybe makes up for too little moisture in a dish. Or, even worse, they are used to cover up the taste of foods that aren't fresh, or to liven up those that just don't have any taste.

With wholefoods one problem is eliminated. Natural ingredients such as freshly picked vegetables, sweet whole grains, subtly flavoured beans, are full of taste. So why add a sauce at all? To turn them into a complete, nutritionally balanced meal.

The sauces given here are as varied as the ways in which they can be used. Don't be tied by habit – try the recipe you'd expect to serve on vegetables with rice instead, and vice versa. Don't stick religiously to the ingredients listed – adapt them to suit what's in your cupboard or garden. Don't make the sauce too thick – remember, it's meant to complement the other ingredients, not swamp them. Many of them can also be used with pancakes, omelettes, as a topping for pizzas or toast too.

On the subject of toppings, those given here are only to get you started. You can use countless ingredients in countless ways to add crunch and texture to softer base ingredients – make them with wholemeal flour, potato, rolled oats, etc. and they'll go down well with the hungrier members of your family as well as those who put flavour and interest first. Try the recipes here with such base ingredients as vegetables (left-overs, again, can be used), beans, brown rice, millet, lentil stew . . . whatever you have handy. If it's pre-cooked, so much the better, and quicker.

For toppings that don't need to be baked, heat the base ingredients separately, then add the topping and cook for a minute or two under the grill.

Sauces

BASIC WHITE SAUCE
Time: 5 minutes

1 oz (25g) wholemeal flour
½ pint (¼ litre) milk (whole, skimmed or plant milk)
1 oz (25g) polyunsaturated margarine or 1 tablespoonful
   vegetable oil
Pinch of nutmeg or paprika
Seasoning to taste

1. Heat the margarine in a pan, add the flour and stir it until well coated with the fat. Cook briefly on a medium heat.

2. Remove from the heat and pour in the milk, stirring well.

3. Return the pan to the heat and slowly bring the sauce to the boil, using a wooden spoon to ensure it is lump-free as it thickens. Cook a minute more and season.

4. Serve as it is, or adapt the basic recipe in one of the following ways.

Variations:

MUSHROOM SAUCE

Fry 2 oz (50g) of chopped mushrooms and one small chopped onion in the margarine before adding the flour; or substitute a few chopped olives for the onion.

CELERY SAUCE

Fry one finely chopped stick of celery in the margarine before adding the flour; season with celery salt.

EGG AND PARSLEY SAUCE

When the sauce is cooked, stir in one or two chopped hard-boiled eggs and 1 tablespoonful of chopped parsley, plus a dash of soy sauce.

CREAMY MUSTARD SAUCE

Blend 1 tablespoonful of dry mustard with the flour, then proceed as usual, adding a tablespoonful of cream or yogurt to the cooked sauce.

TOMATO SAUCE

Fry a small chopped onion in the margarine before adding the flour, and stir half the contents of a small tin of tomato *purée* into the finished sauce. A tablespoonful of Parmesan cheese can also be added.

ALMOND SAUCE

Brown 1-2 oz (less than 50g) blanched almonds, cut into slivers, in the margarine before adding the flour. For a richer sauce, add 1 tablespoonful of ground almonds with the flour.

CHEESE AND PEPPER SAUCE

Cook a little finely grated pepper in the margarine before adding the flour, then stir 3-4 oz (less than 100g) grated cheese into the cooked sauce.

HERB SAUCE

Add 1-2 tablespoonsful of very finely chopped fresh or dried herbs to the finished sauce – especially good are chervil, tarragon, marjoram, lovage, lemon balm, summer savory.

QUICK HOLLANDAISE SAUCE

Take the cooked sauce off the heat and whisk in an egg plus 1 dessertspoonful of lemon juice. Return to the heat for a few minutes, but do not let the sauce boil.

BASIC BROWN SAUCE
Time: 15 minutes

2 oz (50g) polyunsaturated margarine
1 small onion
1 small carrot
1 oz (25g) wholemeal flour
½ pint (¼ litre) brown stock (or water with 2 teaspoonsful
    yeast extract)
1 teaspoonful mixed herbs
Seasoning to taste

1. Finely chop the peeled onion and carrot, and cook gently
    for 5 minutes in the melted margarine.

2. Stir in the flour and continue cooking for a few minutes
    more.

3. Add the stock, seasoning and herbs and cook until the sauce
    thickens.

4. Serve as it is, or – for a traditional brown sauce – strain to
    remove the vegetables.

TOMATO BASIL SAUCE
Time: 15 minutes

5 large tomatoes
2 tablespoonsful vegetable oil
1 tablespoonful basil
Lemon juice
Seasoning to taste
1 tablespoonful yogurt or soured cream – optional

1. Heat the oil; peel and chop the tomatoes.

2. Cook the tomatoes in the oil with the basil and seasoning.

3. After 10 minutes, remove from the heat, mash the tomatoes to make the sauce smooth and stir in the lemon juice.

4. Add the yogurt or cream and serve immediately.

CHICK PEA SAUCE
Time: 10 minutes

4 oz (100g) cooked chick peas
1 large onion
1 tablespoonful vegetable oil
Garlic salt to taste
1 tablespoonful tahini – optional

1. Slice and lightly fry the chopped onion in the oil.

2. Mash the chick peas (or, better still, use a grinder). Combine with the onion and garlic salt.

3. Add some of the stock in which the chick peas were cooked to get the desired consistency. Stir in the tahini.

YOGURT GARLIC SAUCE
Time: 5 minutes

½ pint (¼ litre) yogurt
1 small garlic clove
Sea salt to taste

1. Mince or crush the garlic.

2. Combine thoroughly with the yogurt and add salt.

3. Chill until needed.

TAHINI AND MISO SAUCE
Time: 10 minutes

1 tablespoonful miso
3 tablespoonsful tahini
1 tablespoonful wholemeal flour
½-¾ pint (275-415 ml) water

1. Mix the miso and tahini together in a saucepan.

2. Put over a low heat and stir in the flour; cook gently for a few minutes.

3. Add the water to make the sauce easy to pour; bring to the boil, then simmer for 5 minutes, stirring frequently.

BLUE CHEESE SAUCE
Time: 10 minutes

1 medium onion
2 oz (50g) mushrooms
2 oz (50g) polyunsaturated margarine
2-3 oz (less than 75g) blue cheese

1. Heat the margarine; gently *sauté* the finely sliced onion and mushrooms.

2. Crumble the blue cheese into the pan and cook, stirring continually, until the cheese melts.

BEAN SAUCE
Time: 10 minutes

4 oz (100g) mixed cooked beans
2 sticks celery
Vegetable stock (or water in which beans were cooked)
1 teaspoonful tarragon
Seasoning to taste
Soy sauce

1. *Purée* the beans in a blender with the finely chopped celery.

2. Tip into a saucepan; add sufficient stock to make the sauce the desired consistency; season to taste and add the herbs.

3. Heat through. If a spicier flavour is required, add some soy sauce.

HOLLANDAISE SAUCE
Time: 10 minutes

2 egg yolks
2 tablespoonsful lemon juice
2-3 oz (less than 75g) butter
½ teaspoonful tarragon
Seasoning to taste

1. Put the egg yolks, lemon juice and seasoning in the top of a double saucepan, (or use a bowl over a saucepan of hot water).

2. Whisk until the sauce starts to thicken.

3. Add the butter, piece by piece, and whisk until dissolved, without letting the sauce come to boiling point.

4. Sprinkle in the tarragon. (If the sauce is too thick, add a little yogurt).

PEA AND CARAWAY SAUCE
Time: 40 minutes

6 oz (175g) green split peas, soaked overnight
⅓ pint (200ml) milk
1 tablespoonful caraway seeds
1 tablespoonful bran
Seasoning to taste

1. Simmer the peas in the water in which they were soaked.

2. When soft, drain the excess liquid from the peas. Combine with the milk, seasoning and seeds. Cook gently, stirring occasionally.

3. Remove from the heat and add the bran.

HAZELNUT CHEESE SAUCE
Time: 5-10 minutes

3 oz (75g) ground hazelnuts
3 oz (75g) grated Cheddar cheese
A little less than ¼ pint (140ml) milk

1. Combine all the ingredients and heat gently until the cheese has melted. Stir frequently.

CURRY YOGURT SAUCE
Time: 10 minutes

1 oz (25g) polyunsaturated margarine
1 medium onion
2 teaspoonsful curry powder (or to taste)
1 tablespoonful wholemeal flour
Seasoning to taste
1 small carton yogurt

1. Melt the margarine and *sauté* the sliced onion until soft.

2. Add the curry powder and cook for a minute or two: add the flour and seasoning and cook for a few minutes more. Stir to keep the paste smooth.

3. Stir in the yogurt and heat gently. Serve at once.

BUTTERMILK SAUCE
Time: 5-10 minutes

½ pint (¼ litre) buttermilk
¼ pint (140ml) yogurt
1 tablespoonful cornflour
Chopped dill or pinch of dried mustard

1. Gently heat together the buttermilk and yogurt.

2. Add the flavouring of your choice.

3. Mix the cornflour in the minimum of water and add to the saucepan. Cook over a low heat, stirring frequently, until the sauce thickens.

VEGETABLE PURÉE

Time: 5 or 20 minutes

1 large onion
2 large carrots
2 large tomatoes } or similar ready-cooked vegetables
2 stalks celery
¼ pint (140 ml) vegetable stock (approximately)
Squeeze of lemon juice
1-2 teaspoonsful mixed herbs
Seasoning to taste

1. Chop the vegetables small and cook with the stock, lemon juice, herbs and seasoning for about 15 minutes.

2. *Purée* in a blender and adjust the seasoning. If using ready-cooked vegetables, heat the sauce gently before serving.

SPICY DHAL SAUCE

Time: 40 minutes

4 oz (100g) yellow split peas, soaked overnight
½ pint (¼ litre) water
1 tablespoonful vegetable oil
1 medium onion
Lemon juice
2 teaspoonsful turmeric
½ teaspoonful cumin seeds
½ teaspoonful coriander
Seasoning to taste

1. Cook the split peas in the water until they are soft enough to mash easily.

2. Meanwhile, heat the oil and gently *sauté* the sliced onion.

3. Add the seeds and cook until they pop, then add the spices and combine thoroughly.

4. Stir together the cooked mashed peas, seeds and spices. Add the lemon juice and any seasoning that is required. Re-heat gently, if necessary.

PEANUT BUTTER SAUCE
Time: 25 minutes

4 oz (100g) peanut butter
½ pint (¼ litre) vegetable stock
1 teaspoonful molasses
1 crushed garlic clove
Squeeze of lemon juice
Paprika

1. Combine the ingredients in a saucepan and place on a low heat.

2. Simmer for about 20 minutes, stirring occasionally.

MAYONNAISE

Time: 10 minutes

1 egg
Sea salt, freshly ground black pepper and pinch of dry
  mustard
1 dessertspoonful lemon juice
¼-½ pint (140-275 ml) vegetable oil
1 dessertspoonful warm water

1. Combine the egg yolk and seasoning in a basin.

2. Beat in the oil, a few drops at a time, until the mixture
   becomes thick. Stop as soon as it seems creamy, or it may
   curdle.

3. Gradually beat in the lemon juice, and then the warm water.

LEMON SAUCE

Time: 5 minutes

Mayonnaise as above
1 dessertspoonful lemon juice
1-2 teaspoonsful finely grated lemon rind

1. Whisk the lemon juice into the mayonnaise.

2. Stir in the rind, making sure it is evenly distributed.

TOFU-PEANUT SAUCE
Time: 5-10 minutes

10 oz (275g) tofu
4 oz (100g) peanut butter, or to taste
Soy sauce
Lemon juice
Seasoning

1. Cut the drained tofu into small pieces, then mash it well, and combine with the peanut butter, soy sauce, lemon juice and seasoning. (You will get a smoother sauce in a shorter time if you have the use of a blender).

Toppings

SAVOURY SESAME CRUMBLE

Time: 30 minutes

4 oz (100g) wholemeal flour
2 oz (50g) polyunsaturated margarine
2 oz (50g) sesame seeds
Seasoning to taste

1. Rub the fat into the flour with the finger tips; stir in the sesame seeds.

2. Sprinkle the mixture over the base ingredients with seasoning.

3. Cook at 375°F/190°C (Gas Mark 5) for 20-25 minutes.

CHEESE AND POTATO SPREAD

Time: 30 minutes

2 large potatoes (cooked left-overs are ideal)
2 tablespoonsful cottage cheese
1 oz (25g) Cheddar cheese
Chopped chives

1. If raw, peel and chop the potatoes, and steam until cooked.

2. Mash them with the cottage cheese, then place over the hot base ingredients.

3. Top with grated cheese and place under the grill for 5-10 minutes, until the potato is heated through and cheese lightly browned. Sprinkle with chives.

GRAIN TOPPING
Time: 15-30 minutes

4 oz (100g) cooked grain (i.e. wheat berries, bulgur, millet)
1 egg
Seasoning to taste
1-2 tablespoonsful Parmesan cheese
Pinch of nutmeg

1. Mix the drained grain, beaten egg and seasoning.

2. Spoon over the base ingredients, press down a little and sprinkle with Parmesan.

3. If the base ingredients are hot, place under the grill for approximately 10 minutes. If cold, cook in the oven at 400°F/200°C (Gas Mark 6) for 20 minutes.

SUNFLOWER WHEAT GERM CRUNCH
Time: 10 minutes

4 oz (100g) wholemeal breadcrumbs
2 oz (50g) wheat germ
2 oz (50g) sunflower seeds
2 oz (50g) polyunsaturated margarine
Garlic salt to taste

1. Heat the margarine and add all the other ingredients.

2. Cook over a low heat, turning often, until the mixture is golden and crisp.

3. Serve sprinkled over the base ingredients, (particularly good with steamed vegetables).

OATMEAL MIX
Time: 15 minutes

4 oz (100g) rolled oats
2 oz (50g) grated cheese
2 oz (50g) polyunsaturated margarine
1 tablespoonful crushed rosemary
Seasoning to taste

1. Rub the margarine into the oats, as if making pastry.

2. Use a knife to blend in the cheese, herbs and seasoning.

3. Sprinkle onto the base ingredients and press down lightly.

4. If the base ingredients are hot, cook under the grill for 10 minutes. If cold, cook in the oven at 400°F/200°C (Gas Mark 6) for 20 minutes.

WALNUT AND CELERY RICE
Time: 10 minutes

3-4 oz (less than 100g) cooked brown rice
2 large sticks celery
2 oz (50g) chopped walnuts
2 oz (50g) polyunsaturated margarine
Chopped parsley
Seasoning to taste

1. Heat the margarine and *sauté* the finely chopped celery for a few minutes, then combine all the ingredients.

2. Cook for a few minutes longer.

3. Cover the base ingredients, press down the rice mixture, and grill under a high heat for a few minutes.

NUT PASTRY
Time: 30 minutes

4½ oz (115g) wholemeal flour
1½ oz (40g) ground brazil nuts
2 oz (50g) polyunsaturated margarine
Cold water

1. Mix the flour and ground nuts together carefully.

2. Rub the margarine into the mixture with the finger tips until it resembles breadcrumbs.

3. Using a knife, blend in as much of the cold water as is needed to form a soft dough.

4. Roll out between two pieces of silver foil; if too crumbly, you may need to add a little more water, re-mould, then start again.

5. Place over the base ingredients, prick with a fork, and bake at 425°F/220°C (Gas Mark 7) for 20 minutes.

TOMATO AND BRAN TOPPING

Time: 15 minutes

2-3 large tomatoes
1 medium onion
1 tablespoonful vegetable oil
2 tablespoonsful toasted bran (or bran cereal)
Soy sauce
Seasoning to taste

1. Heat the oil and fry the sliced onion gently until soft.

2. Add the bran and cook for a few minutes longer. Season, sprinkle with soy.

3. Meanwhile, slice the tomatoes and lay over the base ingredients.

4. Top with the bran mixture. Grill for 5 minutes.

VEGETABLES À LA POLONAISE

Time: 20 minutes

White sauce (see page 31)
4 oz (100g) wholemeal breadcrumbs
3 hard-boiled eggs
1 teaspoonful chopped mint
1 teaspoonful thyme
1 oz (25g) polyunsaturated margarine
Seasoning to taste

1. Make up the white sauce according to instructions.

2. Melt the margarine and gently *sauté* the breadcrumbs until crisp; add the finely chopped eggs, herbs and seasoning, and heat for a few minutes longer.

3. Pour the white sauce over the base ingredients; sprinkle the
    crumb and egg mixture on top.

Note: Although this *polonaise* topping goes especially well with
vegetables, it can also be very tasty with various other base
ingredients. Try it on cooked macaroni or curried rice for a start.

ALMOND CRUMBLE
Time: 30 minutes

4 oz (100g) ground almonds
4 oz (100g) *Weetabix*
4 oz (100g) polyunsaturated margarine
2 teaspoonsful chervil
Seasoning to taste

1. Mix the ground almonds with the crumbled *Weetabix*.

2. Use the finger tips to rub margarine into the nut mixture.

3. Stir in the herbs and seasoning.

4. Sprinkle over the base ingredients; press down lightly. Bake
    at 425°F/220°C (Gas Mark 7) for 20 minutes.

4.

FLASH-IN-THE-PANS

You arrive home from work, shopping, or the tennis court – and you're starving. Don't just turn to the biscuit tin. Throw a few things into a pan instead, cook for just a few minutes, add some kind of flavouring and a dollop of protein – and you've got the makings of a delicious, nutritious, filling meal in minutes.

The secret is to keep a full fridge and an open mind. Just about anything can be turned into a very edible something if you are adventurous enough. With some fresh vegetables, left-over (or simply pre-cooked) grains or beans, cheese and eggs, you're off to a good start. Such wholefoods don't need to be cooked for long – in fact, you'll detract from their nutritional value rather than add to it if you over-cook them. They also don't need to be dished up with a whole lot of trimmings – such time-consuming fancifulness is only necessary when the basic ingredients are lacking (although it can, of course, be fun when you want to impress guests).

You can also cook some very impressive dishes on the cooker top and the recipes you'll find on the following pages cater for these as well as for those you want to spend the absolute minimum of time preparing. The choice is yours. Just remember the one golden rule of cooker top cookery – don't have the heat too high. It's very tempting when you're in a hurry, and when you *seem* to be in control of the situation, to think you can speed things up this way, but you can't. Few recipes call for a lot of heat and most ingredients will lose their valuable vitamins and minerals as well as their taste! Always treat wholefoods with the respect they deserve, and you'll get so much more from them. In every way.

BEAN SPROUT FRITTERS

Time: 10 minutes

1 cupful mung bean sprouts
1 cupful wholemeal breadcrumbs
1 large onion
1 tablespoonful vegetable oil
½ teaspoonful herbs
Soy sauce
Seasoning to taste

1. Chop the onion finely.

2. Combine all the ingredients together well, using enough soy sauce to make the mixture stick together. If you need to use a good amount, you won't need to add salt.

3. Shape into fritters and shallow fry on both sides.

GRILLED COURGETTES
Time: 10 minutes

1 lb (450g) courgettes
1 oz (25g) polyunsaturated margarine
4 oz (100g) cheese
Pinch of paprika

1. Melt the margarine. Cut the courgettes in half lengthwise and brush with the melted margarine.

2. Place them cut-side down on a grilling pan and cook briefly on a high heat so that the skins begin to brown.

3. Turn the courgettes and top with the grated cheese. Sprinkle each with a little paprika. Grill until the cheese bubbles.

Variation: This quick and easy recipe can be made more substantial if you add wholemeal breadcrumbs or crushed *Shreddies* to the cheese before grilling.

RICE AND BEAN BURGERS
Time: 15 minutes

8 oz (225g) cooked brown rice
Approximately 4 oz (100g) cooked kidney beans (or others)
1 leek
2 tablespoonsful vegetable oil
Mixed herbs
Soy sauce
Rolled oats
Vegetable oil for frying

1. Heat 2 tablespoonsful of oil and add the finely chopped leek. Cook until transparent.

2. Remove from the heat and mash the beans into the leeks. Then combine this mixture with the rice, herbs and soy sauce. If the mixture is too dry, add some water or stock.

3. Form into burgers and roll in the oats. Fry on both sides.

CABBAGE PANCAKES
Time: 20 minutes

½ small green cabbage
1 medium red pepper
2 oz (50g) polyunsaturated margarine
½ pint (¼ litre) milk and water mixed
4 oz (100g) wholemeal flour
1 egg
Seasoning to taste
Vegetable oil for frying
Tahini, peanut butter or curd cheese

1. Fry the finely chopped cabbage and pepper in the margarine for 5 minutes, taking care they don't burn. Remove them from the pan.

2. Make a pancake batter by mixing a little of the liquid with the flour and egg. Gradually add the rest of the liquid and beat until smooth. Season.

3. Spoon the vegetables into the batter and combine well.

4. Heat a little oil in a large pan and add a few spoonsful of the mixture. Shake gently to spread the mixture across the pan and cook until set underneath.

5. Flip over and cook on the other side. Use up the rest of the batter in the same way.

6. Serve each pancake topped with a spoonful of tahini, peanut butter or curd cheese.

STIR-FRIED VEGETABLES

Time: 15 minutes

1 head Chinese leaves
2 large carrots
4 oz (100g) pumpkin or sunflower seeds
4 oz (100g) cooked peas
4 oz (100g) bean sprouts
Fresh chopped chives
1 tablespoonsful vegetable oil
Soy sauce
Seasoning to taste

1. Using a large, heavy pan, gently roast the seeds for a few minutes until just beginning to brown.

2. Add the oil and chopped chives, cook for a few minutes longer.

3. Shred the Chinese leaves, chop the carrots into thin slices; add the peas and mix together with the seeds.

4. After a few minutes on a medium heat, sprinkle in some soy sauce and season to taste. Cover and cook for 3 more minutes.

5. Stir in the bean sprouts, heat through, then serve.

BRAZIL NUT CAULIFLOWER
Time: 10 minutes

1 large cauliflower
4 oz (100g) brazil nuts
1 oz (25g) polyunsaturated margarine
Approximately 3 tablespoonsful vegetable stock
Seasoning to taste

1. Break the cauliflower into florets and cook briefly in the minimum of water. Better still, steam them.

2. Meanwhile, grind the nuts to a powder in a grinder.

3. Heat the margarine and add the nuts with the seasoning. Cook very gently for a minute or two, then add the stock to give the ground nuts a sauce-like consistency.

4. Drain the cauliflower and serve with the sauce.

MILLET BALLS
Time: 10 minutes

Approximately 8 oz (225g) cooked millet
1 large onion
1 large carrot
1-2 tablespoonsful any left-over green vegetables
2 teaspoonsful mixed herbs
Seasoning to taste
Vegetable oil for frying

1. Slice the onion and carrot as finely as possible. You can use them raw, or fry them briefly in a little oil.

2. Stir the vegetables, herbs and seasoning into the millet.

3. Roll the mixture into small balls and deep-fry in the hot oil. Drain on paper towels before serving.

Variation: You can use left-over rice in place of the millet.

PARSNIP CAKES

Time: 20 minutes

1 lb (450g) parsnips
1 large egg
2 or 3 *Weetabix* or similar
Chopped parsley
1 oz (25g) wholemeal flour
1 teaspoonful mixed herbs
Seasoning to taste

1. Peel the parsnips, cut into small pieces, steam until soft.

2. Mash the cooked parsnips, add the beaten egg, parsley and seasoning. Crumble the *Weetabix* and add sufficient crumbs to make a firm mixture.

3. Shape into cakes and dip them into the remaining crumbs mixed with the herbs.

4. Grill them gently until heated right through.

Variation: These cakes can, of course, also be fried in vegetable oil.

CURRY IN A HURRY
Time: 25 minutes

2 oz (50g) polyunsaturated margarine
1 onion
1 apple
1 medium garlic clove – optional
1-1½ tablespoonsful curry powder
1 oz (25g) wholemeal flour
1 oz (25g) desiccated coconut
¾ pint (420ml) vegetable stock
Seasoning
4 oz (100g) peanuts
1 lb (450g) spinach

1. Melt the margarine. Add the finely chopped onion and apple, minced garlic, curry powder and peanuts. *Sauté* gently until the onion and apple are soft.

2. Stir in the flour, cook briefly, then pour on the stock and bring to the boil. Lower heat and cook until thickened.

3. Meanwhile, cook shredded spinach in the minimum of water until just tender; drain.

4. Add the spinach and coconut to the curry sauce; cook for at least 10 minutes and serve with rice.

Note: The longer any curry sauce is cooked, the better it will taste. Leaving the sauce overnight and then just heating it up when needed also gives the flavours a chance to mingle and ripen. However, a short-cooked sauce will also go down well with most people. The above sauce can be prepared in less than half an hour, but if you can leave it to simmer longer, do so.

Variation: Omit the nuts and spinach and you have a basic sauce that can be used with a whole range of ingredients: assorted vegetables, beans, nuts, lentils, eggs. Stir in some yogurt for a tangy taste.

'LINCOLN STEW'

Time: 25 minutes

¾ pint (420ml) pea soup (left over from previous meal
   or from soup mix)
5 oz (150g) ham-flavoured soya chunks
1 teaspoonful vegetable oil
8 oz (225g) carrots
Seasoning to taste

1.   Hydrate the soya chunks in boiling water to which the oil
     has been added.

2.   In a saucepan, combine the soup, drained soya chunks, and
     chopped carrots; season. Bring to the boil, stir well, then
     cover and simmer for 15 minutes.

3.   Serve with mashed potatoes.

MACARONI LYONNAISE

Time: 20 minutes

8 oz (225g) wholemeal macaroni
2 large onions
4 oz (100g) polyunsaturated margarine

1.   Cook the macaroni in boiling water for about 10 minutes.

2.   Meanwhile, melt a little of the margarine in a pan and add
     the sliced onions; fry gently. Remove the onions.

3.   Melt the rest of the margarine in the pan and add the well-
     drained cooked macaroni. Fry until it begins to brown.

4.   Stir in the cooked onion and cook a little longer.

CAULIFLOWER AND POTATO SAVOURY

Time: 15 minutes

4 medium potatoes, cooked
1 medium cauliflower
2 large tomatoes
¼ pint (140 ml) water in which 1 teaspoonful yeast
   extract has been dissolved
1 oz (25 g) polyunsaturated margarine
Seasoning to taste
Parmesan cheese

1. Break the cauliflower into florets and fry them gently in the melted margarine for a few minutes.

2. Add the water and yeast extract, plus the sliced potatoes and quartered tomatoes. Stir them gently together.

3. Bring the liquid to the boil, then cover the pan and simmer for 5 minutes.

4. Serve with Parmesan cheese.

KASHA WITH COTTAGE CHEESE

Time: 40 minutes

8 oz (225 g) kasha (roasted buckwheat)
1¾ pints (⅔ litre approximately) water
1 large onion
1 large pepper
2 tablespoonsful oil
1-2 teaspoonsful sage
8 oz (225 g) cottage cheese

1. Heat the oil; lightly fry the chopped onion and pepper.

2. Add the kasha and fry for a few minutes longer over a gentle heat.

3. Add the water and sage, bring to the boil, then cover and simmer until the kasha is cooked (approximately 25 minutes).

4. Remove from the heat, leave to stand for 5 minutes more. Serve topped with spoonsful of cottage cheese.

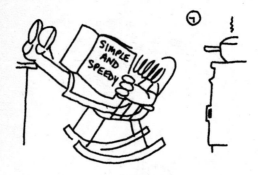

PIPERADE
Time: 10 minutes

(for 2):
1 small green pepper
1 small onion
2 large tomatoes
1 oz (25g) polyunsaturated margarine
4 eggs
Mixed herbs
Seasoning to taste

1. Melt the margarine and lightly fry the chopped pepper and
    onion. Add the sliced tomato and cook for a minute longer.

2. Beat the eggs, season them, then add to the pan in which the
    vegetables are cooking. Stir, whilst cooking gently, until the
    eggs are set. Serve at once.

NOT-SO-PLAIN OMELETTES

Time: 5 to 10 minutes

(for 1):
2 eggs
1 tablespoonful vegetable oil
Seasoning to taste

1. Use a fork to whisk together the eggs, add a tablespoonful water. Season.

2. Heat the oil and, when hot, pour in the eggs. Cook for a minute on a high flame so that the egg mixture sets fairly quickly – lengthy cooking makes it leathery – then lower the heat.

3. Use a spatula to lift the set omelette slightly so that the liquid on top runs underneath.

4. Omelette should be ready within two minutes at the most.

Additions:
A plain omelette made carefully with good fresh eggs is a meal on its own, but additions can change its character completely. Here are some more unusual ideas to try:

Fry cubed wholemeal bread and sliced onion in the oil until lightly browned, then add the beaten eggs and cook as above.

Mix some chopped pepper and a few tablespoonsful of yogurt in with the eggs before adding them to the pan.

Add 1 teaspoonful (or less) of curry powder to the eggs before cooking, and maybe a little cooked brown rice, or sweet corn.

Most vegetables go well with eggs – try adding a little cooked celery, courgettes, cabbage, broccoli, leeks, cauliflower, or bean sprouts.

Add a spoonful or two of wheat germ or bran to the eggs before cooking for extra goodness and fibre; or stir 2 tablespoonsful of yogurt and some mixed herbs in with the eggs.

LEEK PAELLA
Time: 40 minutes

8 oz (225g) leeks
4 medium tomatoes
6 oz (75g) brown rice
2 oz (50g) polyunsaturated margarine
1 pint (½ litre) vegetable stock or water
Seasoning to taste
2 tablespoonsful tahini or 2 oz (50g) toasted flaked
   almonds
Seasoning to taste

1. Remove the outer and wilted leaves of the leeks, cut off the base. Cut into sections about 1 in. long.

2. Melt the margarine, add the leeks and cook gently for 3 minutes, stirring occasionally.

3. Add the rice and fry for a few minutes longer.

4. Stir in the liquid, quartered tomatoes and seasoning. Bring to the boil, cover and simmer until the rice is cooked (approximately 30 minutes).

5. If using tahini, stir it in before serving the rice. Nuts can be sprinkled on top of individual portions.

AUBERGINE 'SANDWICHES'
Time: 10 minutes (excluding draining)

2 round aubergines
6 oz (175g) Cheddar cheese
1 small egg
Wheat germ
1 tablespoonful chopped parsley
Seasoning to taste
A little extra beaten egg
Approximately 2 oz (50g) fresh wholemeal breadcrumbs
Vegetable oil for frying

1. Wash, then cut the aubergines into fairly thin slices; sprinkle with salt and lay on a plate; leave to drain for about 30 minutes.

2. In a bowl combine the grated cheese, beaten egg, parsley and seasoning with just enough wheat germ to make a moist but not too thick paste.

3. Rinse and dry the aubergine slices; sandwich them together with the cheese and egg mixture; dip in beaten egg and then coat well with the breadcrumbs.

4. Deep fry in hot oil until crisp and golden; drain well before serving.

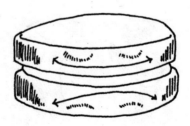

PASTA SHELLS WITH COURGETTES
Time: 15 minutes

8 oz (225g) wholemeal pasta shells
1 lb (450g) courgettes
1-2 oz (25-50g) wholemeal flour
1-2 oz (25-50g) polyunsaturated margarine
2 oz (50g) peanuts
Small carton soured cream
Seasoning to taste

1. Heat a large pan of water, salt lightly, and add the pasta shells; cook gently for about 10 minutes, or until tender but not over-cooked.

2. Meanwhile, slice the courgettes and toss in the flour. Melt the margarine and *sauté* the courgettes, a few at a time so that they are golden, but still crisp.

3. Add the coarsely chopped peanuts and cook for a few minutes more, then stir in the cream and season to taste. Heat through over a low heat for literally a minute or two.

4. Drain and put the pasta shells into a warm serving dish; pour the courgettes and sauce over the top and stir gently. Serve at once.

CAULIFLOWER WITH CREAM
Time: 20 minutes

1 large cauliflower
⅓ pint (200ml) single cream
4 oz (100g) Cheddar cheese, grated
2 oz (50g) wholemeal breadcrumbs
Seasoning to taste

1. Break the cauliflower into florets and steam gently until just tender; transfer to a shallow heatproof dish.

2. Pour the cream over the cauliflower, season well, and scatter with cheese and breadcrumbs.

3. Grill until the cheese melts and the crumbs are golden.

TOFU AND BEAN SPROUTS
Time: 10 minutes

10 oz (275g) tofu
8 oz (225g) fresh bean sprouts
1-2 cloves garlic, crushed
½ red pepper or 1 small pepper
2 tablespoonsful vegetable oil
Soy sauce
Seasoning to taste

1. Drain the tofu well, then cut into cubes. Wash the sprouts, and dry.

2. Heat the oil and gently *sauté* the sliced pepper and garlic until garlic is golden.

3. Add the tofu and bean sprouts, stir well, and cook gently for 3 or 4 minutes only. Season and flavour to taste with soy sauce.

5.

OVEN FARE

Oven cooking is, by its very nature, slow cooking. It takes time for the juices to flow, the flavours to mingle, the crust to turn golden. So why, you ask, put oven fare in a quick cookery book? Isn't that cheating? It isn't, for the simple reason that although something may take longer to cook, that doesn't necessarily mean it takes ages to prepare. What's more, oven cookery can actually save you time and problems in other ways.

If you like to entertain, it can free you to spend more time with your guests and less time fiddling in the kitchen. If you're never quite sure when the people you're cooking for are going to be home, cook the kind of oven fare that will simmer happily until it's needed – and forget it. If you've got free time earlier in the day, but know you're going to be rushed later, prepare your oven fare in advance, and keep it in the cool until the time is right.

Many of the recipes given here are a balanced meal in themselves. To turn them into something more filling, put some bread in the oven just before the dish is ready, and serve them together. Alternatively, add a snappy salad – you needn't spend time on that either, just combine two or three really fresh salad ingredients and serve with a good dressing. And if you want to save even more time, cook double the amount of whatever you're cooking in the oven. Many dishes will keep in the freezer – or try them cold another day; it's amazing how delicious many cooked savouries can taste when they've cooled down.

Finally, do make use of your oven when it's on. In these

energy-conscious days it's wasteful and expensive not to. Cook some simple biscuits or cakes; stew some fruit and, if you don't want it straight away, keep it in a screw-topped jar in the fridge; roast some nuts to use on soups, salads, or to make into nut butters.

DUTCH CHEESE PUDDING
Time: 40 minutes

4 oz (100g) Edam cheese
4 oz (100g) mushrooms
½ pint (¼ litre) milk
1 oz (25g) polyunsaturated margarine
1 large egg
4 oz (100g) wholemeal breadcrumbs
Seasoning to taste

1. Boil the milk, add the margarine and breadcrumbs. Set aside for a few minutes.

2. Meanwhile, wash and chop the mushrooms. (They can be lightly fried if you wish, but can also be used raw).

3. Combine all the ingredients, stir well, and pour into a shallow greased dish. Bake at 425°F/220°C (Gas Mark 7) for about 25 minutes.

AUBERGINE LAYERS
Time: 20 minutes

2 medium aubergines
8 oz (225g) tomatoes
2 oz (50g) flaked or chopped blanched almonds
4 oz (100g) Cheddar cheese
2 teaspoonsful thyme
Seasoning to taste

1. Cook the aubergines in boiling water until tender. Drain, cut off the top and tail, and slice evenly.

2. Slice the tomatoes and grate the cheese.

3. Place a layer of aubergine in a casserole, cover with half the tomatoes, some nuts, cheese and a sprinkling of herbs.

4. Repeat, finishing with cheese and herbs on top.

5. Bake for 10 minutes at 400°F/200°C (Gas Mark 6).

CHICK PEA CASSEROLE
Time: 30 minutes

15 oz (425g) tin chick peas (or equivalent cooked)
½ small cabbage
4 medium tomatoes
2 sticks celery
2 tablespoonsful vegetable oil
1-2 teaspoonsful oregano
Seasoning to taste

1. Heat the oil and gently fry the finely chopped celery and cabbage until just becoming tender.

2. Mix with quartered tomatoes, drained chick peas, herbs and seasoning. Pour into a casserole.

3. Bake for 20 minutes at 350°F/180°C (Gas Mark 4).

POTATO AND WALNUT LOAF
Time: 40 minutes

4 large cooked potatoes (left-overs are ideal)
1 large green pepper
4 oz (100g) walnut pieces
2 eggs
2 teaspoonsful mixed herbs
2 tablespoonsful wholemeal breadcrumbs
½ oz (15g) polyunsaturated margarine
Seasoning to taste

1. Mash the potatoes; chop the pepper finely; beat the eggs.

2. Combine all these with the nuts, herbs and seasoning, and transfer to a lightly greased loaf tin.

3. Top with the breadcrumbs and dot with margarine.

4. Bake at 350°F/180°C (Gas Mark 4) for 30 minutes.

BROAD BEAN CASSEROLE
Time: 45 minutes

1½ lb (675g) broad beans
1 large green pepper
2 sticks celery
2 large carrots
2 tablespoonsful vegetable oil
½ pint (¼ litre) vegetable stock (or water in which beans are cooked)
4 oz (100g) Cheddar cheese
1-2 teaspoonsful mixed herbs
Seasoning to taste

1. Cook the beans in lightly salted water until tender (or cook extra at a previous meal and keep in the fridge until needed).

2. Meanwhile, heat the oil and gently *sauté* the finely chopped pepper, celery and carrots.

3. When tender, mix with the drained broad beans. Add the stock, herbs, seasoning, and 3 oz (75g) of grated cheese. Turn into a greased casserole.

4. Bake at 400°F/200/C (Gas Mark 6) for 20 minutes. Remove from the heat, top with the remaining grated cheese and return to the oven for 5 more minutes.

PEPPER AND SUNFLOWER SEED PIE
Time: 1 hr 10 minutes

4 medium potatoes
2 large peppers
1 large onion
4 oz (100g) sunflower seeds
¼ pint (140ml) vegetable stock
1 teaspoonful yeast extract
Seasoning to taste

1. Peel the potatoes and slice thinly; chop the peppers and onion.

2. Place a layer of potatoes in a pie dish, cover with some chopped pepper and onion, sprinkle with some sunflower seeds.

3. Repeat until all the ingredients are used, finishing with a layer of potatoes. Pour on the stock in which the yeast extract has been dissolved. Season.

4. Bake at 300°F/150°C (Gas Mark 2) for 1 hour.

BAKED SPAGHETTI
Time: 40 minutes

12 oz (350g) wholemeal spaghetti
Approximately 20 green olives
1 lb (450g) tomatoes
1 large onion
2 tablespoonsful cooked sweet corn – optional
8 oz (225g) cream cheese
Water
Seasoning to taste

1. Cook the spaghetti in the usual way.

2. Meanwhile, quarter the tomatoes and olives, and chop the onion as finely as possible. Combine with the sweet corn.

3. Drain the cooked spaghetti; put half in a casserole and cover with half the mixed vegetables. Season. Repeat with the remaining spaghetti and vegetables.

4. Heat the cream cheese gently with enough water to make a pouring consistency. Pour over the casserole ingredients; shake gently so that the sauce infiltrates to the bottom.

5. Bake at 350°F/180°C (Gas Mark 4) for 20 minutes.

BROCCOLI WITH EGGS
Time: 20 minutes

1 lb (450g) broccoli
4 hard-boiled eggs
⅓ pint (200ml) vegetable stock
1 oz (25g) polyunsaturated margarine
2 tablespoonsful Parmesan cheese
Good pinch dried mustard

1. Cook broccoli in a little water, then drain.

2. Put half the broccoli in a casserole, cover with the sliced eggs and finish with the rest of the broccoli. Pour on the stock.

3. Cream the margarine with the cheese and mustard. Spread over the broccoli.

4. Bake at 400°F/200°C (Gas Mark 6) for 10 minutes.

CRACKERS PIZZA
Time: 15 minutes

7 oz (200g) wholewheat crackers
14 oz (400g) tin tomatoes
4 oz (100g) mozarella cheese (or Cheddar)
Garlic salt, oregano, rosemary
1 tablespoonful vegetable oil

1. Lightly grease a shallow dish and cover with half the crackers.

2. Mash the drained tomatoes and add the seasoning and herbs. Spoon half over the biscuits.

3. Add half the cheese. Repeat. Trickle the oil over the top.

4. Bake at 350°F/180°C (Gas Mark 4) for 10 minutes.

BULGUR PILAF

Time: 30 minutes

6 oz (175g) bulgur
2 large leeks
2 large carrots
Approximately 4 oz (100g) cooked split peas or lentils
3 tablespoonsful vegetable oil
½ pint (¼ litre) vegetable stock
Seasoning to taste
Tahini or yogurt to serve

1.   Heat the oil in a large pan. Gently *sauté* the chopped leeks, carrots and bulgur for a few minutes.

2.   Stir in the split peas and stock; season to taste. Transfer to a casserole.

3.   Bake covered at 350°F/180°C (Gas Mark 4) for 15 minutes.

4.   Serve the pilaf with a few spoonsful of tahini or plain yogurt.

ADUKI AND CAULIFLOWER FLAN

Time: 30 minutes

8 oz (225g) *Weetabix* or similar
4 oz (100g) polyunsaturated margarine
1 small cauliflower
4 oz (100g) cooked aduki beans
1 oz (25g) wholemeal flour
1 oz (25g) polyunsaturated margarine
¼ pint (140ml) milk
Seasoning to taste

1. Crush the *Weetabix*, melt the 4 oz (100g) margarine and combine it with the crumbs. Press into a small flan dish taking it up the sides as well as on the base. Set aside to cool.

2. Cook the cauliflower florets briefly in boiling water, drain. Mix with the drained beans.

3. Make a fairly thick sauce by heating 1 oz (25g) margarine, adding the flour and then the milk, and cooking for a few minutes; season.

4. Turn the cauliflower and beans into the sauce, mix well, then place in the prepared flan case.

5. Heat through for 15 minutes at 350°F/180°C (Gas Mark 4).

Variations:
Using the quick flan base above you can make numerous very different flans. Substitute any vegetables, beans, nuts for the ones given. Add grated cheese to the basic white sauce. Gently fry some onions and tomatoes; mix with cooked spinach and finely chopped tofu, and fill the flan case. Combine lightly cooked mushrooms and tomatoes with a spoonful or two of tahini, spoon into the flan base, top with a sprinkling of sunflower seeds. Fill the base with chopped hard-boiled eggs and celery, cover with a layer of grated cheese and wholemeal breadcrumbs. Now try some ideas of your own.

'BACON' HOTPOT

Time: 40 minutes

5 oz (150g) soya 'bacon bits'
2 oz (50g) polyunsaturated margarine
2 large onions
1 large parsnip
2 large carrots
½ pint (¼ litre) vegetable stock
1 bay leaf, seasoning
Fresh parsley

1. Hydrate the soya meat in water.

2. Heat the margarine, add the sliced vegetables and cook gently until lightly browned.

3. Add the drained soya meat and stock plus the bay leaf and seasoning. Transfer to a covered casserole.

4. Bake at 350°F/180°C (Gas Mark 4) for 25 minutes. Serve sprinkled with parsley.

LEEK AND HAZELNUT CASSEROLE

Time: 25 minutes

4 medium leeks
1 small carton soured cream
4 oz (100g) grated cheese
1 oz (25g) wholemeal flour
2 oz (50g) chopped roasted hazelnuts
2 oz (50g) wholemeal breadcrumbs
1 oz (25g) polyunsaturated margarine
Oregano and seasoning to taste

1. Clean the leeks, chop into 1 in. pieces and steam quickly until just soft.

2. Meanwhile, mix the soured cream with the cheese and flour.

3. Drain the leeks and place in a casserole; top with the cheese mixture.

4. Combine the nuts, breadcrumbs, herbs and seasoning with the melted margarine. Sprinkle over the top.

5. Bake at 350°F/180°C (Gas Mark 4) for 10 minutes, or until bubbly.

SWEET CORN PUDDING
Time: 40 minutes

14 oz (400g) frozen sweet corn
2 small cartons yogurt
3 oz (75g) breadcrumbs breadcrumbs
2 oz (50g) grated cheese
1 oz (25g) *Weetabix*
1 egg
1 teaspoonful crushed rosemary
Seasoning to taste

1. Cook the sweet corn in boiling water. Drain.

2. Mix together the corn, yogurt, beaten egg, herbs and seasoning. Spoon into a casserole.

3. Sprinkle crumbled *Weetabix* and cheese over the top.

4. Bake at 400°F/200°C (Gas Mark 6) for 30 minutes.

6.

SNACK HAPPY

Most people's idea of a quick snack is a fry-up. Nutritionally that can mean disaster, although it doesn't necessarily have to. There's a world of difference between soggy tomatoes and fatty processed bread and a plate of mushrooms, tomatoes, free-range eggs and a crisp slice of wholemeal bread, all lightly fried in a pure vegetable oil. (They take the same time to prepare and eat, of course).

But the snacks given here are of a different kind. Salads, for example, are the wholefooder's convenience food, and should be eaten often. They will never be boring, nor time-consuming to prepare, if you keep them simple; use different ingredients from day to day and learn the art of making salad dressings. Try to include a root vegetable with a leafy one, add fresh or dried fruit, nuts or seeds. Almost any vegetable you eat cooked can be eaten raw too – leeks, parsnip, peas, try them all.

Sandwiches are another 'made-in-minutes' snack meal that tend to be all starch and no nutrition. If you've had enough of the polystyrene and paste variety, experiment with some of the ideas given here – then try out some of your own. The only restriction applies when your sandwiches are being taken as part of a packed lunch, in which case it is obvious that too moist a filling is going to make the sandwich too difficult to eat. At home, of course, you can cram in whatever ingredients take your fancy, and if the whole thing starts to fall apart, simply eat it with a fork – or even a spoon!

Given in the following pages are some unusual spreads and

dips. They are also very versatile. The spreads were created to be eaten in sandwiches or on crispbread; the dips taste good with carrots, celery, crackers or crisps. But by cutting back on the liquid content, you can also make a dip into a spread, and vice versa. And dips and spreads all taste great with salad. Once you get the habit of thinking this way, snacks could become your favourite way of eating!

Not-Your-Usual Salads

Slices of orange with finely chopped fennel, some chicory leaves, cucumber chunks, and oil and lemon dressing.

Chopped celery, grated carrot, sultanas and bean sprouts in a yogurt dressing.

Shredded red cabbage, some chopped walnuts, a few grapes, in a French dressing.

Crisp lettuce, diced cheese, watercress and a few chopped dates. A soured cream dressing goes well with this.

Chopped avocado with tomato slices and walnuts in a yogurt dressing.

Sliced raw courgettes, a little finely chopped onion, parsley. Blend yogurt and cottage cheese for the dressing.

Banana slices (tossed in lemon juice) with roasted hazelnuts on a lettuce base.

Cooked wheat berries, chopped pear and bean sprouts in oil and vinegar.

Raw brussels sprouts grated finely and mixed with cherry

tomatoes, green olives and rosemary.

Cold cooked ratatouille makes a delicious salad served on a bed of lettuce. Add some raw peas for protein and texture contrast.

Sweet corn, cucumber slices, red pepper strips and raisins. Any protein-rich dressing goes well with this.

Cold cooked potatoes cut into chunks and mixed with cooked broad beans, some basil, and an oil and vinegar dressing.

A basic cole-slaw (grated cabbage and carrot with mayonnaise) can be varied by the addition of a little crumbled blue cheese, a handful of nuts and raisins, chopped dried apricots, caraway seeds and orange slices, or by changing the dressing – soured cream makes an unusual contrast.

Raw peas and cashews can be mixed with cold cooked curried rice, and served on a lettuce base.

Grapefruit slices and avocado chunks, a sprinkling of sesame seeds, chicory leaves, and tahini dressing.

Chinese leaves, cubed cheese, black olives, with a basil-flavoured dressing.

Raw cauliflower, watercress, chopped apple, tomatoes, and flaked almonds. Try this mixture with a yogurt mayonnaise.

Shredded spinach, some finely chopped onion, hard-boiled egg, and maybe a sprinkling of soya 'bacon bits', in a French dressing.

Raisins, cauliflower, a little chopped raw parsnip, roast cashews, and a tahini dressing. Or try this salad with yogurt in which a few teaspoonsful of curry powder have been mixed.

Red cabbage shredded finely, chopped apple, a few cooked chick peas, lettuce, and a lemon and vegetable oil dressing.

Five-minute Salad Dressings

YOGURT MAYONNAISE

¼ pint (140 ml) yogurt
¼ pint (140 ml) mayonnaise
1 teaspoonful mixed herbs – optional

Stir well together. Keep in the fridge.

PEANUT BUTTER DRESSING

4 oz (100g) smooth peanut butter
½ pint (¼ litre) milk
Pinch of chilli powder or lemon juice and soy sauce

Beat the ingredients until thoroughly blended. Keep in the fridge.

GREEN GODDESS AVOCADO DRESSING

1 medium ripe avocado
1 tablespoonful lemon juice
2 oz (50g) curd or cream cheese
Fresh chives and parsley
Single cream

Mash the avocado with the lemon, then blend in the cheese and finely chopped herbs, with enough cream to make a pouring consistency.

BLUE CHEESE DRESSING

3 oz (75g) blue cheese
¼ pint (140ml) single cream or mild mayonnaise

Crumble then mash the blue cheese; combine well with the cream.

CLASSIC FRENCH DRESSING

2 tablespoonsful vegetable oil
1 tablespoonful cider vinegar or lemon juice
Pinch of dry mustard
Seasoning to taste

Shake or whisk the ingredients together. Vary the taste by adding a crushed clove of garlic, a few crumbled tarragon leaves, some chopped parsley, a pinch of paprika or mixed herbs to taste.

DILL AND YOGURT DRESSING

¼ pint (140ml) yogurt
Soy sauce
Fresh dill
Seasoning to taste

Chop the dill and mix all the ingredients together. You can substitute cottage cheese for the yogurt, preferably blended to a smooth texture first.

CASHEW-NUT DRESSING

4 oz (100g) raw cashew-nuts
Water
Fruit juice

Grind the nuts to a fine powder, add sufficient water to make a thickish paste, then the fruit juice of your choice. This sweet sauce is delicious with most fresh green salads, and is rich in protein.

TAHINI DRESSING

4 oz (100g) tahini
2 spring onions
Water
Seasoning to taste

Add water to the tahini to make it the desired consistency, beat well; stir in the seasoning and finely chopped onions. Leave for a while for the flavours to blend.

SOURED CREAM AND CUCUMBER DRESSING

4 oz (100g) soured cream
1 small cucumber
Lemon juice
Seasoning to taste

Grate the cucumber and mix well with all the other ingredients. For a spicier dressing add a little chilli powder.

EGG DRESSING

2 hard-boiled eggs
1 tablespoonful lemon juice
1 tablespoonful mayonnaise
Chopped parsley
Seasoning to taste
Vegetable oil or extra mayonnaise if needed

Mash the eggs. Combine with the juice, mayonnaise, parsley and seasoning. If the resulting dressing is too thick, thin it down with some oil or extra mayonnaise.

FILLING SANDWICH FILLINGS

Curd cheese with nuts and raisins, mustard and cress
Ripe avocado, a little tahini and bean sprouts
Peanut butter and real fruit jam
Cream cheese with tomatoes, chicory and walnuts
Cottage cheese with slices of fresh peach
Cold cooked beans mashed with yeast extract, herbs and
    cucumber slices
Grated Cheddar cheese, caraway seeds, Chinese leaves
Hazelnut-butter and cole-slaw
Banana, honey and toasted coconut
Mashed hard-boiled egg with green pepper and a little parsley
Miso (mixed with water to make a spread), watercress and tahini
Yeast extract, tomatoes, cheese, mustard and cress
Cottage cheese mashed into mayonnaise with cucumber slices
Cashew-butter and thin slices of apple
Date and cream cheese
Curried avocado with chopped celery and tomato slices
Slices of any tinned nut-meats or left-over nut loaf with crisp
    lettuce
Cream cheese, peanut butter and asparagus

Grated cabbage and pineapple chunks mixed with curd cheese
Cottage cheese, finely grated onion, red pepper, and a pinch of
  coriander.

Spreads and Dips

SUNFLOWER SEED SPREAD
Time: 5-10 minutes

4 oz (100g) ground sunflower seeds
2 oz (50g) peanut butter
1-2 tablespoonsful vegetable oil
Soy sauce

1. Mix together the ground seeds and peanut butter; add
    sufficient oil to get the required consistency.

2. Sprinkle with soy sauce to taste.

CHEESE AND ONION SPREAD
Time: 10 minutes

6 oz (175g) Cheddar or Edam cheese
1 oz (25g) polyunsaturated margarine
1 small onion
Parsley
Seasoning to taste

1. Chop the onion very finely; grate the cheese.

2. Mash all the ingredients together until smooth. If too thin,
    add more cheese; if too thick, blend in a little more
    margarine.

NUTTY LENTIL PÂTÉ

Time: 25 minutes

8 oz (225g) small split red lentils
1 medium onion
2 tablespoonsful vegetable oil
¾ pint (420ml) vegetable stock
1-2 teaspoonsful mixed herbs
3 oz (75g) walnut pieces
Seasoning to taste

1. Heat the oil and gently *sauté* the finely chopped onion. Add the lentils and cook a minute longer.

2. Pour in the stock, seasoning and herbs, bring to the boil and then simmer until all the water has been absorbed.

3. Set aside to cool. Meanwhile, chop the nuts as finely as possible.

4. Mash the lentils to make a thick paste; distribute the nuts evenly and turn into a serving dish. Chill.

GUACAMOLE
Time: 5 minutes

2 large ripe avocados
1 medium onion
1 small green pepper
Squeeze of lemon juice
Pinch of chilli powder and dry mustard
2 tablespoonsful yogurt – optional

1. Mash the avocado to a smooth cream. Add the lemon juice.

2. Chop the onion and pepper as finely as possible and mix into avocado with seasoning to taste.

3. For a smoother guacamole, stir in some yogurt. Chill. As this dip does not keep very well, prepare it shortly before you intend to eat.

BEAN PÂTÉ
Time: 10 minutes

15 oz (425g) tin baked beans
4 oz (100g) Cheddar cheese
2 oz (50g) wholemeal breadcrumbs
1 teaspoonful yeast extract
1-2 teaspoonsful mixed herbs or parsley
Seasoning to taste
Milk to mix

1. Mash the beans and sauce, add the yeast extract and blend well.

2. Grate the cheese and add to the beans.

3. Add the breadcrumbs, herbs and seasoning, plus enough milk to make the pâté the right consistency.

COTTAGE CHEESE DIP

Time: 10 minutes

8 oz (225g) cottage cheese
2 oz (50g) soured cream
1 stick celery
1 small apple or a few dried dates
Seasoning to taste

1. Combine the cottage cheese and soured cream in a blender, or by hand.

2. Finely chop the celery and fruit, and stir into the cheese mixture. Season to taste. If too thick, add a little milk or cream.

3. Chill.

WHEAT GERM YOGURT DIP

Time: 5 minutes

2 oz (50g) wheat germ
2 oz (50g) yogurt
3-4 oz (75-100g) nut-butter

1. Stir together the wheat germ and yogurt.

2. Blend in sufficient nut-butter to make the desired consistency. Combine thoroughly.

CAULIFLOWER SPREAD
Time: 20 minutes

1 small cauliflower
2 oz (50g) tahini
Soy sauce
1 small red pepper
Seasoning to taste

1. Cook the cauliflower florets until soft enough to mash.

2. Add tahini, soy sauce, finely chopped pepper and seasoning; chill.

3. If too thick, add more tahini.

CREAMY WATERCRESS DIP
Time: 10 minutes

1 bunch watercress
4 oz (100g) cream cheese
2 oz (50g) Cheddar cheese
2 tablespoonsful soya 'bacon bits'
Seasoning to taste
A little milk to mix

1. Chop the watercress; grate the Cheddar cheese.

2. Use a fork to combine the cream cheese and Cheddar, then mix in the watercress, 'bacon bits' and seasoning. If the dip is too thick, add a little milk; chill.

Hot Snacks

NUT BURGERS
Time: 10 minutes

4 oz (100g) ground nuts
4 oz (100g) wholemeal breadcrumbs
Seasoning to taste
A little milk

1. Combine the nuts and breadcrumbs; season.

2. Mix in just enough milk for the mixture to stick together.
    Form into burger shapes.

3. Lightly fry for a minute on each side.

CRISPY SCRAMBLED EGGS
Time: 10 minutes

4 eggs
2 oz (50g) polyunsaturated margarine
2 oz (50g) wholemeal breadcrumbs
Chopped parsley
Seasoning to taste

1. Heat the margarine, add the breadcrumbs and parsley, fry
    until the crumbs are crisp.

2. Pour in the beaten eggs and seasoning and cook gently,
    stirring continually.

MUSHROOMS WITH YOGURT SAUCE

Time: 15 minutes

8 oz (225g) mushrooms
1 small pepper or onion
1 oz (25g) polyunsaturated margarine
1 oz (25g) wholemeal flour
Just under ¼ pint (140ml) yogurt
Seasoning

1. Gently *sauté* the sliced mushrooms and pepper in the margarine for 5 minutes.

2. Add the flour and cook for a minute longer, then stir in the yogurt and seasoning.

3. Cook gently for 3 or 4 minutes until the sauce thickens. Serve on toast.

JACKET POTATOES

Time: 30-45 minutes

2 small potatoes (for each person)

1. Wash and dry the potatoes, prick with a fork and cook until just softening.

2. Make a cross in each potato, top with one of the following fillings:

   Cottage cheese and chives; scrambled eggs and mushrooms; a spoonful of tahini and bean sprouts; baked beans; fried onion and pepper with grated cheese; soured cream and chopped onion; sweet corn and a knob of butter or poly-unsaturated margarine; left-over ratatouille; fresh chopped herbs in yogurt; any thick soup that is handy; left-over curry sauce with nuts.

CAULIFLOWER COTTAGE CHEESE
Time: 10 minutes

1 small cauliflower
1 small carton cottage cheese
Pinch of paprika

1. Steam the cauliflower florets until just tender; drain.

2. Spread the cottage cheese over the top, sprinkle with paprika and grill for a minute or two until the cheese is hot.

CREAMED ONIONS
Time: 15 minutes

1 lb (450g) onions
1 oz (25g) peanut butter
1 teasponful yeast extract or soy sauce
Chopped parsley
Seasoning to taste

1. Chop the peeled onions fairly small and cook in the minimum of water for 10 minutes.

2. Stir the peanut butter into the onions so that it dissolves, then add the yeast extract and seasoning.

3. Serve with parsley on toast or a bed of brown rice.

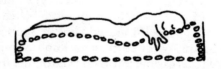

WELSH RAREBIT

Time: 15 minutes

4 slices wholemeal toast
1 oz (25g) polyunsaturated margarine
1 oz (25g) wholemeal flour
¼ pint (140ml) milk
4 oz (100g) Cheddar cheese
Pinch of dry mustard

1. Melt the margarine, add the flour and cook briefly; pour in the milk and cook until a smooth sauce is made. Add the seasoning.

2. Add the cheese and heat until it melts.

3. Spread the sauce on the toast, top with a little extra grated cheese and brown under the grill.

Variations:
Place some lightly steamed or *sautéed* vegetable on the toast before adding the sauce – leeks, celery, mushrooms, sweet corn, tomatoes, onions, all taste good.

Mix some cooked aduki beans, lentils or split peas into the sauce before pouring onto toast.

Vary the cheese and you'll vary the flavour – or try a combination.

When cooked, top your welsh rarebit with a poached or fried egg; or sprinkle on some chopped nuts.

PASTA AND PEAS
Time: 15 minutes

6 oz (175g) wholemeal noodles (or any quick-cooking pasta)
4 oz (100g) fresh or frozen peas
Parmesan cheese
1 oz (25g) polyunsaturated margarine
Seasoning to taste

1. Cook the pasta and peas together in a saucepan of boiling water; they should be cooked enough to eat in about 10 minutes.

2. Drain; toss in margarine and season. Serve with Parmesan cheese sprinkled over top.

FRIED SANDWICHES
Time: 5 minutes

8 slices wholemeal bread
1 small tin nut-meat or 4 oz (100g) Cheddar cheese
1 egg
A little milk
Seasoning
2 oz (50g) polyunsaturated margarine
4 tomatoes

1. Make 4 sandwiches using either thinly sliced nut-meat or cheese for the filling.

2. Whisk the egg, add a little milk and season. Brush the bread with this mixture.

3. Fry each sandwich until golden and crisp in the melted margarine. Top with sliced tomato.

TOMATO SOYA BEANS
Time: 10 minutes

1 14 oz (400g) tin soya beans (or previously cooked beans)
4 large tomatoes
1 stick celery
1 large onion
2 oz (50g) polyunsaturated margarine
2 teaspoonsful oregano
Seasoning to taste

1. Open the tin of beans, drain off the sauce.

2. Gently fry the chopped vegetables in the melted margarine for 6 or 7 minutes.

3. Tip in the beans, add the seasoning and herbs and heat through.

7.

TAKING POT LUCK

There's nothing new about the idea of cooking everything together in one pot. In fact, primitive tribes managed to survive for centuries on a diet of root vegetables, herbs, some grains, occasionally a little meat, all of it stewed for hours in a pot hung over a fire. It may not have been very varied, but it probably tasted pretty good. One-pot cookery does enable a number of not-so-exciting ingredients to blend their flavours, sometimes with quite amazing results. Just think what you can do with the great variety of fresh ingredients available today!

There are other advantages in one-pot cookery. If you're not too skilful at timing the cooking, simmer it all together and you won't go wrong. If you are short on saucepans, or simply hate cleaning them, one-pot cookery has obvious advantages.

All the following concoctions can be cooked in a casserole, or a heavy saucepan with a well-fitting lid. No times have been indicated because they can be cooked for as long as you like – that's the advantage of them. Throw everything into the pot, and forget about them. A pressure cooker will, of course, speed up the cooking process, but in general these are recipes for the cook who doesn't want to spend long in the kitchen preparing the food, but doesn't mind waiting whilst it all cooks to perfection.

There is one other way you can cook in one pot, a way that saves electricity and gas. Use a wide-necked Thermos flask (and slow-cooking items like beans could well become a delicious staple in your house). Cooking this way is a slow process, but once you've done the preparations you can forget all about your meal until you're ready for it. Then unscrew the top, and your food is ready to serve. Thermos cookery is a new idea, but one that's catching on fast. The most important point is to remember that the water or stock you add must be boiling hot – and the flask top firmly sealed.

All the recipes given here can be cooked in a casserole in the oven, on top of the cooker, or in a thermos flask. You can cut the preparation time by eliminating the *sautéeing* of certain ingredients before adding them to the rest, and just putting everything in together – *sautéeing* seals the surface and holds in the flavour, so makes your food just that little bit tastier, but it isn't absolutely necessary.

WHEAT BERRY STEW

8 oz (225g) wheat berries, soaked overnight
2 large onions
2 large carrots
2 large green peppers
4 oz (100g) small red lentils
1 teaspoonful basil
2 tablespoonsful vegetable oil
Seasoning to taste

1. Heat the oil and gently *sauté* the drained berries and chopped vegetables, stirring frequently.

2. Add the lentils and cook for a minute or two longer.

3. Put all ingredients into a container, add the seasoning and herbs. Cover with boiling water, seal, and leave until wheat berries are tender.

POT-AU-FEU

8 oz (225g) beef-flavoured soya 'meat' chunks
3 leeks
1 small cauliflower
2 oz (50g) brown rice
4 oz (100g) fresh or frozen peas
1 tablespoonful vegetable oil
2 large tomatoes
Pinch of cayenne pepper and rosemary
2 bay leaves
Seasoning to taste

1. Hydrate the soya meat in boiling water to which the oil has been added.

2. Chop the leeks, break the cauliflower into florets.

3. Combine the soya meat with the leeks, cauliflower, rice, peas, herbs and seasoning. Turn into a container and cover with boiling water (include the stock in which the soya meat was soaked).

4. Seal, and leave until all the ingredients are cooked. Stir in the quartered tomatoes just before serving.

BANANA RISOTTO

8 oz (225g) brown rice
1 large onion
1 tablespoonful vegetable oil
Pinch of cumin
2 oz (50g) cashew nuts
3 medium bananas
1 small green pepper

1. Heat the oil, lightly *sauté* the sliced onion.

3. Stir the rice into the oil and onion mixture, add the cumin, then transfer to a container and cover with boiling water.

3. Seal and leave to cook.

4. Just before serving, mix in the nuts and banana chunks and garnish with thinly sliced pepper.

MUSHROOM GOULASH

1 lb (450g) mushrooms
1 medium onion
1½ oz (40g) polyunsaturated margarine
5 tablespoonsful water
2 medium tomatoes
1 small carton yogurt
Pinch of paprika
Seasoning to taste
Fresh parsley

1. Melt the margarine; *sauté* the sliced onion for a few minutes, then add the sliced mushrooms and cook for a few minutes longer.

2. Add the water, paprika, quartered tomatoes, and mix gently. Heat thoroughly, then transfer to a container.

3. Seal and leave to cook for a short time only.

4. Stir in the yogurt, adjust the seasoning and serve, sprinkled with parsley.

BARLEY AND VEGETABLE STEW

4 oz (100g) pot barley
1 large onion
1 large carrot
2 large sticks celery
4 oz (100g) yellow split peas, soaked overnight
2 tablespoonsful vegetable oil
Seasoning to taste

1. Roast the barley in a dry pan until just beginning to brown.

2. Chop the onion, carrot and celery and *sauté* briefly in oil. Add barley and *sauté* for a few minutes longer.

3. Stir in the peas, add seasoning, plus enough water to cover.

4. Bring to the boil then turn into a container and seal. Cook until barley is soft.

Variation: Replace the barley with millet for a quicker-cooking casserole.

BEAN FEAST

8 oz (225g) mixed small beans (i.e. aduki, mung, lentils, split peas), soaked overnight
Approximately 1½lb (675g) of any vegetables in season (i.e. green beans, broccoli, parsnips, carrots, leeks, peppers, etc.)
2 teaspoonsful yeast extract
1 tablespoonful vegetable oil
1 tablespoonful mixed herbs

1. Drain the beans, peel and chop the vegetables.

2. Put the beans and vegetables into a container. Dissolve the yeast extract in a little drop of boiling water and add it to the beans.

3. Pour in sufficient boiling water to cover all the ingredients, add the herbs and seasoning, seal. Leave until cooked.

BUCKWHEAT WITH MISO

6 oz (175g) buckwheat
2 large onions
1 large green pepper
1 tablespoonful vegetable oil
2 oz (50g) peanuts
2 oz (50g) fresh bean sprouts
Approximately 1 teaspoonful miso

1. Dry-roast the buckwheat until beginning to brown.

2. Lightly *sauté* the sliced onions and pepper in the oil for a few minutes.

3. Add the buckwheat and cook for a minute more, then pour on enough water to cover the ingredients and bring to the boil.

4. Transfer to a container, seal and leave to cook.

5. When almost ready to eat, take a little of the liquid from the container and mix it with the miso. Return it to the container with the bean sprouts and peanuts for a few minutes more.

IRISH HOTPOT

1½ lb (675g) potatoes
½ medium cabbage
2-3 large onions
3 large carrots
4 oz (100g) peas, fresh or frozen
Water or vegetable stock
4 oz (100g) Cheddar cheese
Seasoning to taste

1. Scrub or peel the potatoes, cut them into small pieces. Peel and slice the onions and carrots, chop the cabbage.

2. Put all the ingredients into a container with the peas and enough water to just cover everything. Seal and leave to cook.

3. Season to taste and serve with the grated cheese.

8.
QUICK BREADS, BISCUITS AND CAKES

Home baking is synonymous with all those delightful old-fashioned ways of passing time – which is enough to put anyone who has a family, a job, hobby or better things to do with their time off for good! Baked goods are, however, a mainstay of most people's diets. And if you're honest, you have to admit that it often takes as long to go down to the shops when you run out of bread or cake as it would to bake your own.

Making bread the traditional way is, of course, a lengthy job, though well worth the effort if you've got a freezer and can do a large batch at a time. But why be a traditionalist? Bread may be the staff of life, but don't lean on it too heavily. There are plenty of quick breads and savoury biscuits that can be cooked at home in no time, and that make a delicious alternative to bread. They may be heavier or crunchier, or difficult to slice – but they'll go just as well with your breakfast honey, or lunch-time soup. Try them – you'll love them.

The following recipes for biscuits and cakes are only a small sample of the many quick-to-make varieties you can indulge in once you get the idea. In fact, most traditional types of recipes can be adapted to use wholefoods – just replace white flour with wholemeal, refined sugar with the raw kind, some of the butter with low-cholesterol polyunsaturated margarine. As wholemeal flour absorbs more moisture, you may need to add a little extra. You may also have to forget how you think things *should* taste and start enjoying how they *do* taste – if the ingredients are fresh and wholesome, you can't really go wrong.

Speed up the preparation of your baking by eliminating, whenever possible, such fussing as chopping things up small, mixing things one at a time; do not be afraid to judge quantities rather than measure them precisely. Use small dried fruits (raisins, currants) rather than large. Buy pre-chopped nuts, or nut pieces and use them as they come. Try the all-in-one mixing method – it usually works well, even when not specified. Use shallow tins rather than deep ones and cut your cake into bars rather than slices.

QUICK RYE BREAD
Time: 20 minutes

8 oz (225g) wholemeal rye flour
2 teaspoonsful baking powder
2 teaspoonsful raw cane sugar
⅓ pint (200ml) milk with 2 tablespoonsful skimmed milk
  powder added
2 oz (50g) melted polyunsaturated margarine
Pinch of sea salt

1. Combine the flour, baking powder, sugar and salt.

2. Pour in the milk and melted margarine and stir to make a smooth dough.

3. With floured hands, place on a well greased baking sheet, then gently press down to make a circle about ½ in. thick. Prick dough with a fork.

4. Bake at 450°F/230°C (Gas Mark 8) for 10 minutes. Cut into wedges.

CUMIN CRACKERS
Time: 20-25 minutes

8 oz (225g) plain wholemeal flour
4 oz (100g) polyunsaturated margarine
Approximately 5 tablespoonsful milk
2 teaspoonsful ground cumin
Pinch of sea salt

1. Sift together the flour, cumin and salt, then rub the margarine into the dry ingredients to make a crumb-like mixture.

2. Add just enough milk to bind to a dough.

3. Roll the dough out as thinly as possible on a floured board and cut into squares, strips or rounds.

4. Arrange on a lightly greased baking sheet and bake at 400°F/200°C (Gas Mark 6) for 10-15 minutes, or until cooked.

CHAPATTI

Time: 20 minutes

8 oz (225g) wholemeal flour
Sea salt to taste
Water

1. Sift the flour and salt together, then add enough water to form a soft but not sticky dough.

2. Knead on a well floured board for 5 to 10 minutes, or until completely elastic and smooth in texture.

3. Break the dough into small pieces, form into balls, roll each one into a large thin round.

4. Heat a heavy frying pan or griddle and cook each *chapatti* for barely a minute, flip over and cook for a minute longer.

5. Stack in a tea-towel to keep them warm whilst you cook the rest.

6. Traditionally served with curry, *chapatti* make a quick and delicious substitute for bread.

CARAWAY CHEESE FINGERS

Time: 20 minutes

8 oz (225g) wholemeal flour
4 oz (100g) polyunsaturated margarine
8 oz (225g) grated Cheddar cheese
Approximately 2 oz (50g) caraway seeds
Seasoning to taste
Pinch of paprika

1. Cream together the softened margarine and grated cheese.

2. Add the flour and seasoning.

3. Roll out pastry until ¼ in. thick and cut into fingers.

4. Sprinkle with seeds and a little paprika.

5. Bake at 375°F/190°C (Gas Mark 5) for about 10 minutes until crisp and golden.

Variation: Instead of caraway seeds, make these savoury biscuits with sesame or poppy seeds, or top with flaked nuts.

IRISH SODA BREAD
Time: 40 minutes

8 oz (225g) wholemeal flour
1 teaspoonful bicarbonate of soda
1 egg
1 tablespoonful honey
⅓ pint (200ml) milk
Pinch of sea salt

1. Stir together the flour, bicarbonate of soda and salt.

2. Beat the egg, add the honey and milk.

3. Carefully combine all the ingredients, then knead lightly to work in all the flour and make a smooth dough. Add more milk if too dry, flour if too wet.

4. Make a large ball of the dough and place on a greased baking sheet. Flatten out to a circle, and use a knife to make a cross about ½ in. deep on the top.

5. Bake at 375°F/190°C (Gas Mark 5) for 30 minutes or until the loaf is brown. Test by tapping the bottom of the loaf – when cooked it will sound hollow. Cool on a wire rack.

KARINTO (Deep-fried Cookies)
Time: 15 minutes

8 oz (225g) wholemeal flour
2 oz (50g) sesame seeds (raw or roasted)
Water
Sea salt to taste
Vegetable oil for frying

1. Mix the flour and seeds together and add the salt.

2. Pour on enough water to form a soft dough and knead briefly.

3. Roll into a sausage shape and use a sharp knife to cut into small thin rounds.

4. Fry quickly in hot oil until crisp, then remove from the heat and drain on a paper towel. Eat hot or cold, or store in an air-tight container.

LEMON HONEY BISCUITS
Time: 25 minutes

5 oz (150g) wholemeal flour
3 oz (75g) polyunsaturated margarine
1 oz (25g) raw cane sugar
2 oz (50g) honey
1 tablespoonful lemon juice
Finely chopped lemon peel – optional

1. Beat together the margarine, sugar and honey until creamy smooth.

2. Work in the flour and lemon juice, add the peel.

3. With damp hands, form the dough into small balls and place on a greased baking sheet. Flatten slightly.

4. Bake at 350°F/180°C (Gas Mark 4) for 15 minutes.

MUESLI MUNCHIES
Time: 25 minutes

4 oz (100g) polyunsaturated margarine
6 oz (175g) raw cane sugar
1 large egg
4 oz (100g) self-raising wholemeal flour
4 oz (100g) oats and/or cereals such as barley and rice flakes
2 oz (50g) raisins
2 oz (50g) chopped nuts, raw or roasted
A little milk

1. Cream together the margarine and sugar, then add the egg and stir well.

2. Mix in the flour, a little at a time.

3. Gradually add all the remaining ingredients with enough milk to make a batter.

4. Drop tablespoonsful of the mixture onto greased baking sheets, leaving room for the biscuits to spread.

5. Bake at 350°F/180°C (Gas Mark 4) for 10-15 minutes.

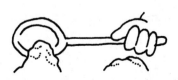

EASY EASTER BISCUITS

Time: 25 minutes

8 oz (225g) wholemeal flour
4 oz (100g) polyunsaturated margarine
4 oz (100g) raw cane sugar
2 teaspoonsful mixed spice
6 oz (175g) currants
A little milk

1. Cream the margarine and sugar together, then add the sifted flour and spice.

2. Stir in the currants.

3. Mix in enough milk to make a dough.

4. Roll out to about ¼ in. thick and cut into large rounds.

5. Place on a lightly greased baking sheet and cook at 325°F/ 170°C (Gas Mark 3) for about 15 minutes.

HONEY AND WHEAT GERM FLAPJACKS

Time: 25 minutes

3 oz (75g) polyunsaturated margarine
3 oz (75g) honey
5 oz (150g) oats
1 oz (25g) wheat germ
Pinch of sea salt

1. Melt the margarine and honey together gently in a saucepan.

2. Stir in the oats, wheat germ and salt, making sure they are well blended.

3. Spread the mixture evenly in a greased and floured 7 in. tin, and press down lightly.

4. Bake at 350°F/180°C (Gas Mark 4) for about 20 minutes, or until turning gold.

5. Mark into portions while still warm, and remove carefully when cool but not completely cold.

APRICOT CRISPS
Time: 20 minutes

4 oz (100g) self-raising wholemeal flour
1 oz (25g) cornflour
2 oz (50g) polyunsaturated margarine
1 oz (25g) raw cane sugar
Dried apricot pieces

1. Sift together the flour and cornflour, then rub the margarine into the dry ingredients.

2. Stir in the sugar.

3. Knead lightly until you can form the mixture into balls. Place them on a lightly greased baking sheet, leaving room to spread; top each with a piece of dried apricot.

4. Bake at 375°F/190°C (Gas Mark 5) for 10 to 15 minutes, until crisp.

Variations: Other kinds of dried fruit go well with these tasty biscuits, as do nuts.

SPICY SOYA BISCUITS
Time: 20 minutes

6 oz (175g) soya flour
4 oz (100g) honey
1 egg
4 oz (100g) raw cane sugar
2 oz (50g) polyunsaturated margarine
2 teaspoonsful baking powder
1 teaspoonful mixed spice

1. Cream together 2 oz (50g) of the sugar and the margarine.

2. Separate the egg; add the yolk and most of the white to the sugar mix.

3. Beat in the honey.

4. Sift the flour and baking powder, stir into the mixture, and knead to blend thoroughly.

5. Roll the dough as thinly as possible, brush with the lightly beaten egg white, sprinkle with the remaining sugar mixed with the spice.

6. Cut into required shapes, put onto baking sheet, and bake at 350°F/180°C (Gas Mark 4) for 10 to 12 minutes.

GRIDDLE CAKES
Time: 15 minutes

8 oz (225g) self-raising wholemeal flour
1 teaspoonful baking powder
1 oz (25g) polyunsaturated margarine
1 tablespoonful honey
2 eggs
Approximately ⅓ pint (200ml) milk

1. Sift together the flour and baking powder; rub in the margarine.

2. Make a well in the centre and add the eggs and honey with a little of the milk.

3. Gradually beat in the rest of the milk until the mixture will just drop from a spoon.

4. Lightly grease a griddle or thick-based frying pan, and heat until it makes a drop of water sizzle.

5. Drop dessertspoonsful of the batter well apart on the hot griddle, and cook until the bubbles rise to the surface (approximately 3 minutes).

6. Turn the cakes and cook for 3 minutes more.

7. Whilst using the rest of the batter, keep the cooked cakes wrapped in a tea-towel to prevent them becoming dry. Eat with butter and jam.

PEANUT BUTTER BARS
Time: 10 minutes

8 oz (225g) wholemeal digestive biscuits
2 oz (50g) polyunsaturated margarine
4 oz (100g) crunchy peanut butter

1. Crush the digestive biscuits.

2. Mix with the melted margarine.

3. Whilst still warm, stir in the peanut butter and make sure all ingredients are thoroughly blended.

4. Turn into a lightly greased shallow tin and press down; chill.

5. When set, cut into even-sized bars.

YOGURT SCONES
Time: 20 minutes

8 oz (225g) wholemeal flour
1½ teaspoonsful baking powder
1 oz (25g) polyunsaturated margarine
5 oz (150g) carton plain yogurt
Pinch of sea salt

1. Sift together the flour, baking powder and salt.

2. Rub in the margarine.

3. With a spoon, add the yogurt, stirring to make a soft dough.

4. Knead for a minute or two, then roll out to about ½ in. thickness and cut into rounds.

5. Arrange on a greased baking sheet and cook in the oven at 400°F/200°C (Gas Mark 6) for 12 minutes.

BANANA MUFFINS
Time: 30 minutes

6 oz (175g) wholemeal flour
2 oz (50g) raw cane sugar
1½ oz (40g) polyunsaturated margarine
2 teaspoonsful baking powder
1 egg
⅓ pint (200ml) milk
1 large ripe banana

1. Cream together the margarine and sugar.

2. Add the beaten egg and mashed banana.

3. Stir in the milk.

4. Sift together the flour and baking powder and add to the mixture.

5. Beat the batter for a few minutes to lighten.

6. Half fill some well greased, warmed patty tins and bake at 375°F/190°C (Gas Mark 5) for about 20 minutes, or until firm. Eat hot or cold.

ROCK BUNS
Time: 20 minutes

8 oz (225g) self-raising wholemeal flour
4 oz (100g) polyunsaturated margarine
4 oz (100g) raw cane sugar
4 oz (100g) mixed dried fruit
1 egg
A little milk

1. Rub the margarine into the flour.

2. Beat the egg, then add it to the flour; mix with the sugar and fruit. Combine well.

3. Pour in just enough milk to make the mixture sticky but still quite firm.

4. Use two spoons to put rounds of the mixture onto a greased baking sheet, leaving room for spreading.

5. Bake at 400°F/200°C (Gas Mark 6) for 10 to 15 minutes, or until you can press the buns and not leave a mark.

6. Leave to cool a little before removing from the baking sheet.

HONEY NUT SQUARES

Time: 35 minutes

4 oz (100g) plain wholemeal flour
1 teaspoonful bicarbonate of soda
2 oz (50g) raw cane sugar
4 oz (100g) honey
1 large egg
2 tablespoonsful vegetable oil
1 teaspoonful mixed spice
1 teaspoonful cinnamon
2 oz (50g) flaked almonds
Pinch of sea salt

1. Sift together the flour, bicarbonate of soda, spices and salt.

2. Add the sugar and honey; beat the egg and oil together and stir into the mixture (if too dry, add a little milk).

3. Grease a small square baking tin and pour the mixture into it. Smooth the top and sprinkle with the nuts.

4. Bake at 375°F/190°C (Gas Mark 5) for 25-30 minutes, and cut into squares when cool.

GINGER SULTANA BARS
Time: 10 minutes (preparation)

8 oz (225g) wholemeal ginger biscuits
4 oz (100g) sultanas
2 tablespoonsful honey
2 oz (50g) polyunsaturated margarine

1. Crush the biscuits into small but not too even crumbs.

2. Melt the margarine with the honey, then stir in the crumbs, making sure they are all well coated with the mixture.

3. Press into a shallow Swiss roll tin and set aside to firm up; cut into bars.

MOLASSES ROCK CAKES
Time: 30 minutes

10 oz (275g) self-raising wholemeal flour
4 oz (100g) polyunsaturated margarine or butter
2 oz (50g) raw cane sugar
2 oz (50g) raisins
2 eggs
2 tablespoonsful molasses
Extra raw cane sugar for topping

1. Rub the fat into the flour to make a breadcrumb-like mixture; stir in the sugar and raisins.

2. Stir in the beaten eggs and molasses and combine the ingredients thoroughly.

3. Drop spoonfuls of the mixture onto a greased baking sheet leaving room to spread; sprinkle with extra sugar; bake at 400°F/200°C (Gas Mark 6) for about 15 minutes or until firm to touch. Leave to cool briefly on the tray before transferring to a wire rack.

9.

DESSERTS

The quickest and easiest dessert to serve is fresh fruit, a favourite not just with wholefooders, but with slimmers, gourmets, children, picnickers – most people, in fact. But, in fairness, it must be admitted that it can become a little boring, especially in winter when the variety is limited (and the quality is not always what it should be).

So what else can you dish up to cheer up your family? Yogurt is another obvious choice. Forget about the over-sweetened supermarket variety and either buy or make your own plain yogurt, to which you can add a wide range of ingredients to ring the changes – fresh, stewed or dried fruit, nuts, honey, molasses, maple syrup, wheat germ, crunchy oat cereal, raw sugar jams, candied peel, crushed biscuits, lemon curd ... What's more, you can mix it with whipped cream for a low-calorie topping, stir it into pancake batter, blend it with milk and fruit for a long cool drink, make a high-protein custard or a delicious ice cream, or add it to the batter for fruit fritters. Yogurt is as versatile as it is nutritious, and is invaluable to the wholefooder in a hurry.

Amazingly, you can also conjure up quick sweets from left-over unflavoured savouries. For example, plain brown rice can be put into the blender with chunks of banana, a handful of raisins, and maybe some honey to make an unusual cream dessert. Left-over wholewheat berries can be heated up with a little cream, flavoured with some chopped apple and a few walnuts. Cooked millet is good with fruit *purée*. Stale wholemeal bread can be made into crumbs, lightly fried in polyunsaturated margarine, sweetened with raw cane sugar and used as a crunchy topping.

More elaborate desserts can take time to prepare, especially when the look of the dish is as important as its taste. And for those very special occasions, time spent in this way is well worth while. If, however, you just don't have the time to spare, you can still produce some interesting and unusual dishes. Take a look at the recipes that follow – they are just a small example of what can be done. None of them take much of your precious time in preparation, though they might need to be left to soak, chill or set.

SUMMER PUDDING
Time: 15 minutes (preparation)

1½ lb (675g) summer fruit (traditionally a combination of
  such fruits as red- or blackcurrants, raspberries,
  cherries, rhubarb)
4 oz (100g) honey
6-8 slices wholemeal bread

1. Wash the fruit, put into a saucepan, and cook gently with the honey until just tender.

2. Meanwhile line a *soufflé* dish with the bread, cutting it as necessary to make sure there are no gaps.

3. Spoon in the fruit and juice so that it holds the bread in place.

4. Place a layer of bread on top of the fruit, then cover with a saucer or small plate weighted down to press on the bread.

5. Chill for at least 8 hours, preferably longer, so that the juices have time to soak through the bread. Turn out and serve on its own, or with yogurt, cream or custard.

NO-COOKING LEMON SOUFFLÉ
Time: 10 minutes (preparation)

¼ pint (140ml) whipping cream
1 packet agar-agar lemon jelly
1 egg
Grated rind and juice of a lemon
1 orange

1. Make up the jelly using just under ¾ pint (420ml) of liquid (the lemon juice plus water).

2. Separate the egg and whisk the yolk into the jelly mixture, add the grated rind, and set aside to cool.

3. When it begins to firm up, stir in the stiffly beaten egg white and whipped cream, pour into a *soufflé* dish, and leave to set completely.

4. Decorate with orange slices before serving.

APPLE CRISP
Time: 20 minutes

Approximately 1½ lb (675g) cooking apples
4 oz (100g) raw cane sugar, or to taste
1-2 teaspoonsful mixed spice
Pinch of ground cloves
1 oz (25g) polyunsaturated margarine
3 oz (75g) rolled oats
2 oz (50g) honey

1. Combine the cored, peeled and sliced apple with the sugar, spices and a little water; cook until soft.

2. Meanwhile, melt the margarine in a separate pan, blend in the honey and then the oats, making sure they are well coated.

3. Transfer the apple to a flat dish, top with the oat mixture, and grill for 2 or 3 minutes until oats are crisp. Serve hot.

COEUR À LA CRÈME
Time: 5 minutes (preparation)

8 oz (225g) cream cheese
2 oz (50g) plain yogurt
8 oz (225g) fresh raspberries or strawberries
2 oz (50g) raw cane sugar

1. Blend the cheese and yogurt until smooth.

2. Pack into a mould (a heart shape is traditional); chill for at least 2-3 hours.

3. Tip from the mould onto a serving plate, garnish with the fruit and sprinkle with sugar.

STEWED PRUNES WITH PEAR
Time: 30 minutes

8 oz (225g) prunes
4 medium pears
¼ pint (140ml) water
¼ pint (140ml) pure fruit juice
2 tablespoonsful raw sugar apricot jam
2 tablespoonsful honey

1. Wash the prunes, then leave them to soak overnight in the water and fruit juice.

2. Peel and core the pears, cut into thin slices, and put into a saucepan with the prunes and other ingredients.

3. Cook gently, stirring occasionally until the fruit is soft.

4. Eat hot or cold.

CHOCOLATE MOUSSE
Time: 10 minutes

4 oz (100g) raw sugar chocolate
2 egg whites
2 tablespoonsful pure orange juice

1. Grate the chocolate and melt it slowly in a saucepan or double boiler with the orange juice, then set aside to cool.

2. Beat the egg whites until stiff and fold into the chocolate mixture.

3. Spoon into four glasses and chill thoroughly before serving.

CARROT MUESLI
Time: 10 minutes

4 oz (100g) rolled oats
¼-½ pint (140-275 ml) milk
1 tablespoonful molasses (or to taste)
2 large carrots
Pinch of ginger

1. Combine the oats, milk and molasses, to make a muesli of the consistency and sweetness desired.

2. Grate the carrots very finely.

3. Stir the carrots into the muesli, season with a little ginger, serve immediately.

DRIED FRUIT SYLLABUB (in blender)
Time: 10 minutes

4 oz (100g) dried apricots
4 oz (100g) dried peaches
½ pint (¼ litre) pure orange juice
½ pint (¼ litre) single or whipping cream
2 oz (50g) flaked almonds (raw or roasted)

1. Soak the fruit in the juice overnight.

2. Put the fruit and juice in a blender to make a smooth *purée*.

3. Whip the cream and fold into the *purée*.

4. Spoon into four glasses and top with flaked almonds.

YOGURT PANCAKES
Time: 10 minutes

1 small carton plain yogurt
1 egg
2 oz (50g) 81 per cent wholemeal flour (or 100 per cent)
Pinch of sea salt
Lemon juice
Raw cane sugar to taste

1. Whisk the beaten egg into the yogurt, then add the salt and the flour; (if using 100 per cent wholemeal, sieve it first).

2. Heat a little oil in a small pan and spoon in some of the mixture; cook gently, then turn and cook the other side until golden.

3. Continue until you have used all the batter, then serve pancakes with lemon juice and sugar to taste.

SEMOLINA WITH FRUIT AND NUTS
Time: 15 minutes

4 oz (100g) wholewheat semolina
3 oz (75g) polyunsaturated margarine
⅔ pint (400ml) milk
4 oz (100g) raw cane sugar
1 oz (25g) raisins
1 oz (25g) almonds or walnuts

1. Heat 1 oz (25g) of the margarine and gently fry the raisins and chopped nuts for a few minutes, then set aside.

2. Melt the rest of the butter, add the sugar and semolina and cook for a few minutes more; then pour in the milk very slowly, stirring continually.

3. Cook gently, still stirring, until the mixture thickens and the semolina is ready.

4. Pour into bowls that have been rinsed in cold water, leave to cool; top with the fruit and nuts before serving.

PINEAPPLE FRUIT SALAD
Time: 10 minutes

1 medium-sized fresh pineapple
Approximately 1 lb (450g) fresh fruit
2 tablespoonsful Kirsch or 2 tablespoonsful honey and
   1 tablespoonful lemon juice

1. Carefully remove the top of the pineapple and then the flesh.

2. Cut this into chunks and mix with other fresh fruit of your choice; sprinkle with Kirsch or the combined honey and lemon juice.

3. Spoon the fruit back into the pineapple shell and chill.

4. Serve the fruit directly from the pineapple at the table.

LEMON YOGURTS
Time: 5 minutes

1 pint (½ litre) plain yogurt
4 good tablespoonsful raw sugar lemon curd
Raw sugar chocolate – optional

1. Stir the lemon curd into the yogurt and mix thoroughly. Chill for an hour if possible before serving.

2. Divide between four glasses or dishes, and top with a little flaked chocolate.

APRICOT TOFU PURÉE (in blender)
Time: 5 minutes

8 oz (225g) dried apricots, soaked overnight
12 oz (350g) tofu
Squeeze of lemon juice
2 oz (50g) flaked almonds, roasted or raw

1. Drain the apricots and cut them into chunks; drain the tofu.

2. Combine them with the lemon juice and whizz in a blender to make a golden, creamy sauce.

3. Serve at once (or chill briefly) topped with the nuts.

Note: Virtually any dried or fresh fruits can be used with tofu in this way; if they are not sweet enough, add a little honey or maple syrup. Examples to try: banana, prunes, strawberries, pineapple, apple *purée* with raisins.

CHRISTMAS SHORTBREADS

Time: 5 minutes

8 rounds of wholemeal shortbread
4 tablespoonsful raw sugar mincemeat
¼ pint (140 ml) double or whipping cream
1 oz (25 g) roasted flaked almonds

1. Sandwich the shortbread with the mincemeat to make 4 portions.

2. Top each with a generous dollop of whipped cream and scatter with a few nuts. Best made just before you intend to serve them.

INDEX